The First Book of Sopr

COMPLETE
Parts I, II, and III

ISBN 978-1-4803-3321-5

Complete Package released 2013

G. SCHIRMER, *Inc.*

www.musicsalesclassical.com
www.halleonard.com

THE FIRST BOOK OF SOPRANO SOLOS

PART I

PREFACE

Repertoire for the beginning voice student, whether teenager, college student, or adult, always poses a great challenge for the voice teacher because of the varied abilities and backgrounds the students bring to the studio. This series of books for soprano, mezzo-soprano and alto, tenor, and baritone and bass provides a comprehensive collection of songs suitable for first and second year students of any age, but is compiled with the needs of the young singer in mind.

In general, students' first experiences with songs are crucial to their further development and continued interest. Young people like to sing melodious songs with texts they can easily understand and with accompaniments that support the melodic line. As the student gains more confidence, the melodies, the texts, and the accompaniments can be more challenging. I have found that beginning students have more success with songs that are short. This enables them to overcome the problems of musical accuracy, diction, tone quality, proper technique, and interpretation without being overwhelmed by the length of the song.

Each book in this series includes English and American songs, spirituals, sacred songs, and an introduction to songs in Italian, German, French and Spanish. Many students study Spanish in the schools today, and most studio volumes do not include songs in this language; therefore, we have included two for each voice type.

Several songs in the collections have been out of print in recent years, while others have been previously available only in sheet form. Special care has been taken to avoid duplication of a great deal of general material that appears in other frequently used collections. These new volumes, with over thirty songs in each book, are intended to be another viable choice of vocal repertoire at a very affordable price for the teacher and student.

Each book contains several very easy beginning songs, with the majority of the material rated easy to moderately difficult. A few songs are quite challenging musically, but not strenuous vocally, to appeal to the student who progresses very rapidly and who comes to the studio with a great deal of musical background.

In general, the songs are short to medium in length. The ranges are very moderate, yet will extend occasionally to the top and the bottom of the typical voice. The majority of the accompaniments are not difficult, and are in keys that should not pose major problems. The variety of texts represented offers many choices for different levels of individual student interest and maturity.

In closing, I wish to thank Richard Walters at Hal Leonard Publishing for allowing me to be part of this effort to create this new series of vocal collections. We hope that these books will fill a need for teachers and students with suitable, attractive and exciting music.

Joan Frey Boytim

CONTENTS

THE BEATITUDES

Matthew 5:3-6

Albert Hay Malotte

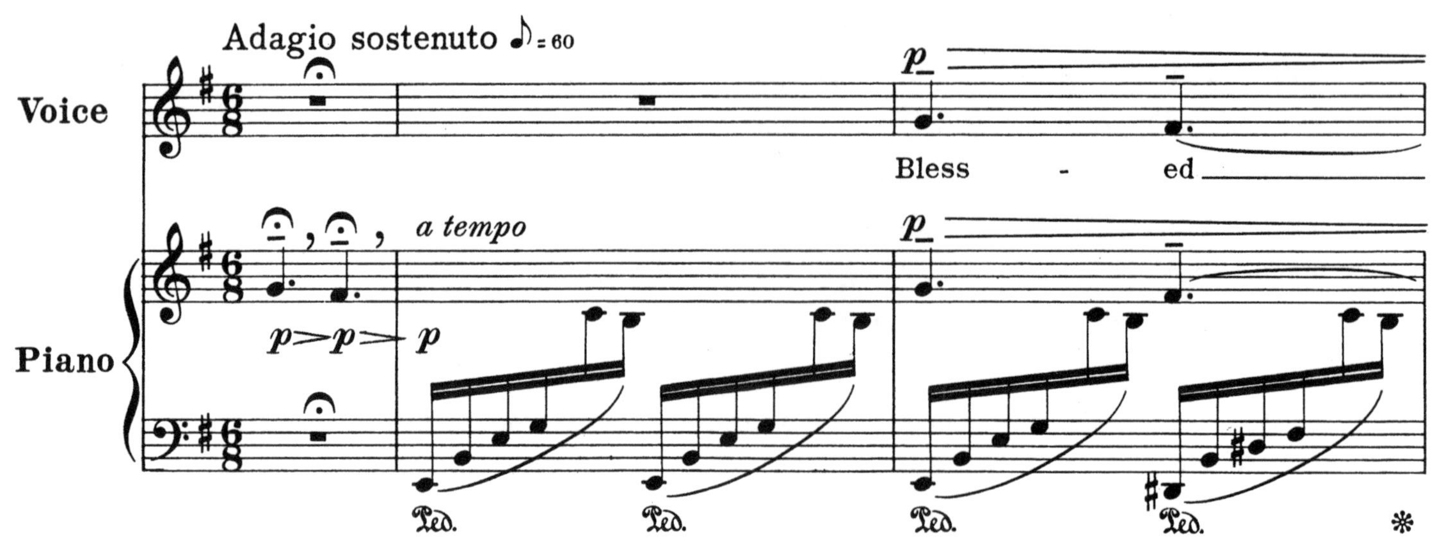
Adagio sostenuto ♪ = 60
Voice
Piano
a tempo
p
Bless - ed

rit.
a tempo
are the poor in spir - it:

p
mf
rit.
cresc.
for theirs is the king - dom of heav - -

ten.
mp
en.
p
Bless - -
ten.
p
espr.
mp
ten.
ed are they that mourn: for they shall be
rit.
p
rit.
pp
com - - fort - ed.
ten.
pp
pp
ten.
ral - len - tan - do
p
pp
morendo
Ped.
p
Ped.
Ped.
Ped. sostenuto

Lento assai ♩= 50
rit.
p
rit.
a tempo
p
Bless - - ed are the meek: for
a tempo
p
they shall in - her - it the earth.
rit.
Ped.
Ped.
*

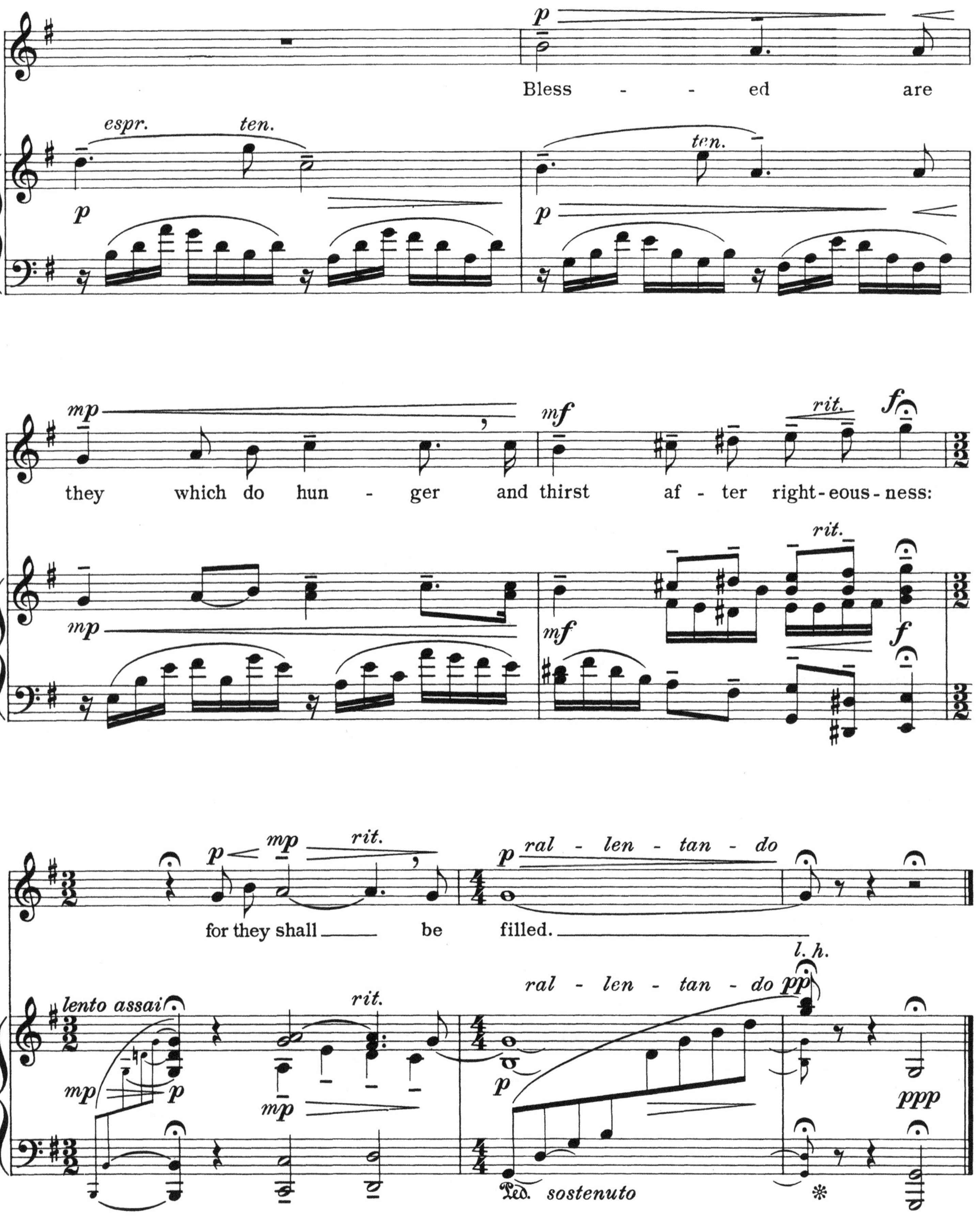

p
Bless - - ed are
espr. ten.
p
ten.
p

mp
they which do hun - ger and thirst af - ter right-eous-ness:
mf
rit.
f
mp
mf
rit.
f

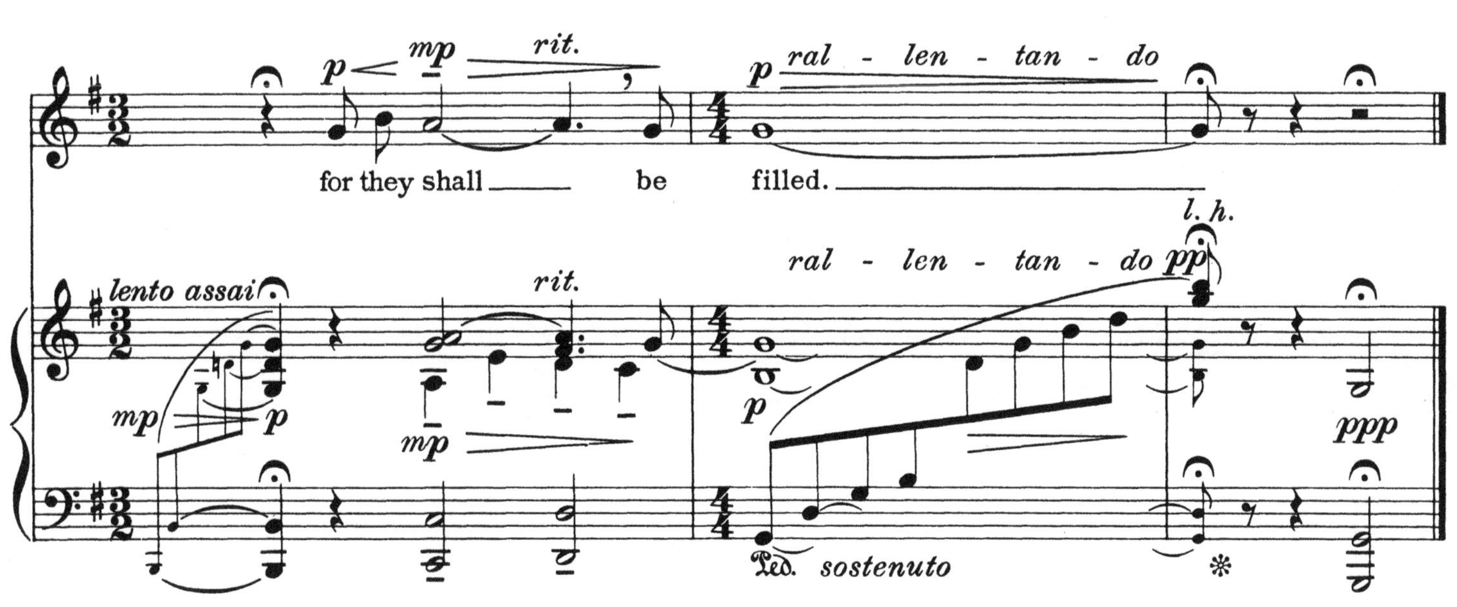

BEL PIACERE

Bel piacere è godere fido amor!
questo fà contento il cor.
Di bellezza non s'apprezza lo splendor
se non vien d'un fido cor.

To enjoy a devoted love
brings contentment to the heart.
If there is no faithful heart,
there is no beauty, no wisdom, and no fascination.

George Frideric Handel

fi - do a - mor! bel pia - ce - re
è go - de - re fi - do a - mor!
mf
que - sto fà con - ten - to il cor, que - sto fà con -
ten - to il cor, fa con - ten - to il cor,

que - sto fà con - ten - to il cor, que - sto
fà con - ten - to il cor, fà con -
ten - to il cor.
Fine

Di bel - lez - za non s'ap - prez - za lo splen - dor,
p
se non vien d'un fi - do cor, d'un fi - do cor;
di bel - lez - za non s'ap - prez - za lo splen - dor,
tr
se non vien d'un fi - do cor, d'un fi - do cor.
mf

D.S. al fine

BONNE NUIT
(Good Night)

Jules Massenet

Andantino.
p
La ter - re dort au ciel pur, Les é -
The sleep-ing earth si-lent lies 'Neath the
dolciss.
pp 2 Ped.
toi - les dans l'a - zur_ De-scend-ent veil - ler sur el - le; Sur_ ter - re
tran-quil a - zure skies, O'er her stars their guard are hold - ing; On the earth what
un jar-din fleu-rit Mais les fleurs ont_ pli - é l'ai - - -
bloom - ing gar-dens rise, But the blos-soms soft their wings are fold - - -
dim.
le. Bon - ne nuit, bon - ne nuit, bon - ne nuit!
ing. Sweet good night, sweet good night, sweet good night!
pp

Un pe-tit toit mon-te seul Au jar-din sous le til-leul,
A lit-tle cot, scarce 'tis seen, Hides a-mid a gar-den green,
Il porte une hum-ble tou-rel-le, Un oi-se-let dans son nid
It bears an hum-ble wee tow-er, Where a bird-ling watch-es o'er the scene
dim.
Ga zouille et fait sen-ti-nel - - - le. Bon-ne
Twit-t'ring in its leaf-y bow - - - er: Sweet good
nuit, bon-ne nuit, bon-ne nuit!
night, sweet good night, sweet good night!
pp

Dans la tou - relle une en - fant S'est en - dor - mie en rê - vant
This tow - er holds, hap - py nest, A sleep - ing child, sweet - ly blest,
A la fleur frai - che comme el - le, Le ciel la garde et re-luit
Dreams she of the flow'rs al - so sleep - ing, May Heav'n, re - flect-ed in her breast,
dim.
En son â - me jeu-ne et bel - - le. Bon - ne nuit, bon - ne
From all harm her young life be keep - - ing! Sweet good night, sweet good
nuit, bon - ne nuit!
night, sweet good night!
pp

EL TRA LA LA Y EL PUNTEADO

Es en balde, majo mío,
Que sigas hablando,
Porque hay cosas que contesto
Yo siempre cantando.
Por mas que preguntes tant,o,
En mi no causas quebranto,
Ni yo he de salir de mi canto.

*It's no use, my majo,**
For you to keep trying,
Because there are times when I answer
Always with a song.
Keep on pestering me,
You cannot upset me.
I will continue singing my song.

** majo is an untranslatable word for a dashing, handsome lover*

Enrique Granados

blan - do, por que hay co - sas que con - tes - to yo siem - pre can - tan - do.
al Coda
Tra la la la la la la la la la la la la la la la la la.
p
Por mas que pre - gun - tes tan - to.

Tra la la la la la; en mi no cau - sas que -
bran - to ni yo he de sa - lir de mi can - to
D.S. al Coda
la la la la la la. Es -
CODA

THE CRUCIFIXION

from The Speckled Book, 12th century
translated by Howard Mumford Jones*

Samuel Barber

*From *Romanesque Lyric*, by permission of the University of North Carolina Press.

f
broadly
Ah, sore was the suff-'ring borne By the bod-y of Ma-ry's
f
p tenderly and slower
Son, But sor-er still to Him was the grief Which for His
p
mf
p
sake Came up-on His Mo - ther.
Tempo I allarg.
espr.
mf
p
mp

EL MAJO DISCRETO
(My Discreet Sweetheart)

F. Periquet
translated by Olga Paul

Enrique Granados

que a - mor es de - se - o que cie - ga y ma - re - a ha
For true love is blind when the flow-ers are in sea - son, I
tiem - po que sé que quien á ma - no vé.
touch him and oh, I know I love him so!
p
Mas si no es mi - ma - jo un
And if his looks are not so
hom - bre, que por lin - do des - cue - lle y a - som - bre
pleas - ing, I still won - der a - bout all this teas - ing,

En cam-bio͜ es dis - cre - to͟ y guar-da͜ un͟ se - cre - to que
Since he knows dis - cre - tion,͟ A se - cret in his pos - ses-sion Re -
y po - sé en el͟ sa - bien - do͟ que es fiel.
mains be - tween just us,͟ He's nev - er͟ friv-o - lous!
p
¿Cual es el se - cre - to que͜ el ma - jo guar -
What is͟ the se - cret my sweet-heart has to

do? Se - ri - a — in-dis - cre - to con - tar - lo yo, No
keep? To — tell — is — in-dis - creet, It —— is so deep! And
po - co — tra - ba - jo cos - ta - ra — sa - ber se - cre - tos de un
too, it — would be quite a task to — un - furl The — se-crets of a
ma - jo con —— u - na mu - jer. Na - ció en La - va -
lov - er and —— his on - ly girl. He's much bet - ter than the
pies. ¡Eh! ¡Eh! Es un ma - jo un ma - jo es.
rest, Oh! Oh! He's the man whom I love best.

EVERYWHERE I LOOK

Molly Carew

cro - cus call'd 'good - bye' to him, And the vi - o - let from her nook; For
p
Spring is here in shoes of green,
f
Ev - 'ry - where I look.
p
f
f
rall.
a tempo
Spring is here, Spring is here, Ev - 'ry - where I
rall.
a tempo
look!
mf
This
sf dim.
Ped.
* Ped.
*

morn-ing, in the mer-ry, mer-ry woods, The trees with laugh-ter shook! They'd
con espressione
seen Love steal my heart from me- My hap-py heart he took! I
a tempo
legato
colla voce
a tempo
did not heed, but let it go And sang with bird and brook, For
cresc.
cresc.
Spring is here in shoes of green, Ev-'ry-where I look! Ha,

rall.
Ha, ha, ha, ha, ha, Ha, ha, ha, ha, ha, ha, This
rall.
mf a tempo
morn-ing, in the mer-ry, mer-ry woods, The trees with laugh-ter shook! They'd
mf a tempo stacc.
seen old Win-ter hob-ble past A-lean-ing on his crook. The
cro-cus call'd 'good-bye' to him, And the vi-o-let from her nook; For

p
f
f
Spring is here in shoes of green, Ev-'ry-where I look! Spring is here!
ff a tempo
Spring is here, Ev-'ry-where I look, Ev-'ry-where I look,
colla voce
Spring is here! Spring is here, Wher-e'er I look!
a tempo
fff a tempo
sf

THE GREEN DOG

words and music by
Herbert Kingsley

mp
on it.
Shoes of leaf - green,
Hose of tea - green, Coat of ap-ple - green, Gloves of bottle - green,
In fact, I nev - er would be seen
ex - cept in
8
mf
rit.
a tempo
green
If my dog were green.
rit.
a tempo
f

But, a - las! no mat - ter what you've heard, The facts are con - sis - tent - ly ab -
surd,
For my dog is - n't green,
And, what sets the mat - ter e - ven more a - gog—
I have - n't an - y dog!
l.h.
l.h.
l.h.
ff
mf
colla voce
fff

HAVE YOU SEEN BUT A WHITE LILY GROW

Ben Johnson

Anonymous, time of James I

swan's down ev-er? Or have smelt of the bud of the bri-ar? Or the
nard of the fire? Or have tast-ed the bag of the bee? O so white, O so
soft, O so sweet is she, so sweet is she; O so
white, O so soft, O so sweet, so sweet,_ so sweet is she.
p
p

HEAR MY CRY, O GOD

César Franck

Andantino, quasi lento
mp
cresc.
poco rit.
f
dim.
p
a tempo
p
Hear my cry, O
God, at - tend un - to my prayer; From the end of the earth

pp
will I cry un - to Thee, When my heart is o - ver - whelm'd,
pp
cresc.
lead me to the Rock that is high - er than I, that is
cresc.
f
dim.
p
mf
high- er than I. For Thou hast been a shel - ter for me and a strong
dim.
tower a strong tower from the en - e - my.
poco rall.
a tempo

poco rit.
p
When I cry unto God
then shall my en - e -
p a tempo
mies turn back; this I know, for God is for
me. In God will I praise His word, In
cresc.
cresc.

f largamente
God I have put my trust,
In God will I
f colla voce
a tempo
più f
praise His word.
Let my mouth be fill'd with
a tempo
più f
praise,
and with Thy hon - or all the day.
largamente
p
largamente
mf a tempo
poco rall.
A - - men,
A - - men.
mf a tempo
poco rall.
rall.

HEFFLE CUCKOO FAIR

Rudyard Kipling

Martin Shaw

U.K. Sole Selling Agents:
WILLIAM ELKIN MUSIC SERVICES, Station Road Industrial Estate, Salhouse, Norwich NR13 6NY, England
New York: G. Schirmer Inc., Sole Agents for U.S.A.

Tell him squat and square - a! Old Wo-man! Old Wo-man! Old
Wo-man's let the Cuc-koo out At Hef-fle Cuc-koo Fair - a!
March has search'd and A-pril tried —
'Tis-n't long to May now, Not so far to Whitsun-tide, And Cuckoo's come to stay now!

mf
Hear the va-liant fel - low shout Down the or-chard bare - a!
Old Wo-man! Old Wo-man! Old Wo-man's let the Cuc-koo out At
f
f
Hef-fle Cuc-koo Fair - a!
mf
When your heart is young and gay And the sea - son rules it-
8va

Work your works and play your play Be-fore the Au-tumn cools it! Kiss you turn and
turn a-bout, But my lad, be-ware - a! Old Wo-man! Old
Wo-man! Old Wo-man's let the Cuc-koo out At Hef-fle Cuc-koo Fair - - - a!
Without slackening time.
8va

THE K'E

from the Chinese, 718 B.C.

Celius Dougherty

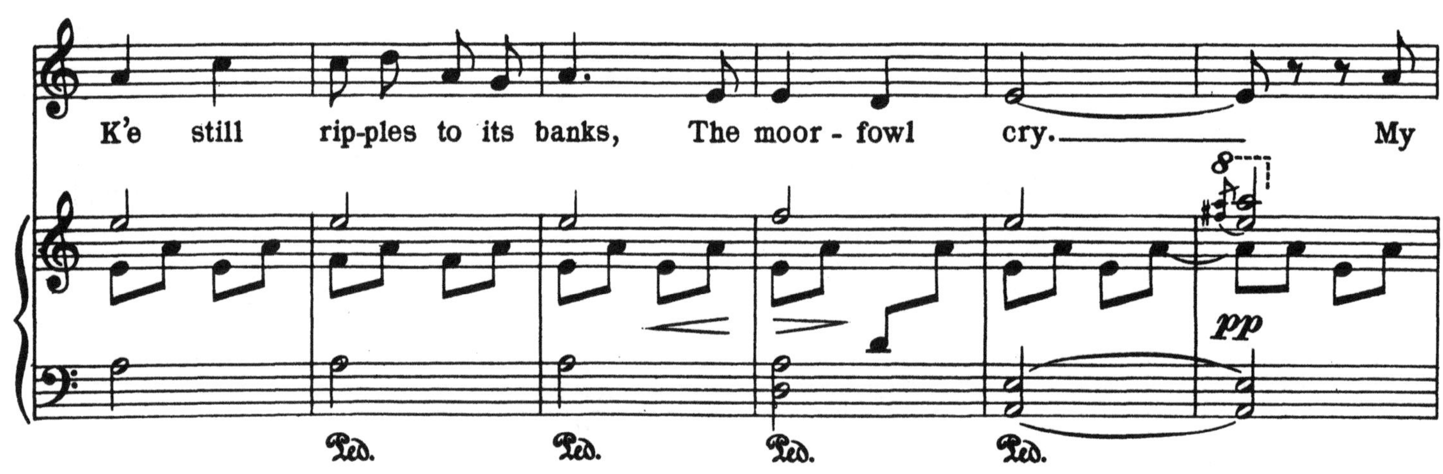

*Pronounced *kay*

mp
Sell - ing of silks you were, A lad not of our
kin; You passed at sun-set on the road From
far - off Ts'in.
The
f
rit.
p

slowly again
frogs were croak-ing in the dusk; The grass was wet. We
pp
Ped.
talked to-geth-er, and I laughed; I hear it yet.
mf
p
f more moving
I thought that I would be your

wife; I had your word. And so I
took — the — road with you, And cross the
cresc.
8
ford. I do not
f
lunga
p slowly
lunga
pp

know when first it was your eyes looked cold.
But
Ped.
rit.
all this was three years a - go,
And
rit.
dim.
pp
I am old.
ppp
rit.

I LOVE ALL GRACEFUL THINGS

Kathleen Boland

Eric H. Thiman

* Available in Key G. Curwen Edition 71977

London: J. Curwen & Sons Ltd., 29 Maiden Lane, W.C.2
New York: G. Schirmer Inc., Sole Agents for U.S.A.

swan that glides up - on the lake, The rip - ple of the flow - ing stream, The
cir - cle of the swal - low's flight, The clouds that al - most move - less seem.
The rise and fall of sil - v'ry waves, The
flut - t'ring wings of but - ter - flies, The curv - ing scythe a -

mong the corn, The set - ting sun, when day - light dies. The au - tumn dance of
with - er'd leaves, The snow-flakes stea - dy, gen - tle fall, The
gleam - ing slant of A - pril rain, I love them all, I love them all,
poco meno mosso
cresc.
a tempo
semplice
I love them all.
rall.

INTO THE NIGHT

words and music by
Clara Edwards

mf
there. I turn my gaze toward the
dolce
mf
morn - ing sun As from the east he comes_ thro' the dark and the
mf
dew; The flow - ers lift their heads– the night is gone– But
mf
mf
where are you? The
dolce

mf
count - less wea - ry steps I do not heed Tho' they be
o - ver land or bound - less sea; I care not where the road may
f
f
lead If I but come a - gain at last to thee.
mf
l.h.
mf
dim.
p
Si - lent - ly in - to the night I go, In - to the
p

mf
star - ry night of heav - en - ly blue; What mat - ters where the road may
mf
lead If I but come a - gain at last to you!
l.h.
p
p
pp
Si - lent - ly, si - lent - ly
pp
ppp
rit.
I come to you!
rit.
morendo

LET MY SONG FILL YOUR HEART

words and music by
Ernest Charles

it's sub - lime!
Let my song say the
words
That my lips are a - fraid to say—
Of the
yearn - ing
And of de - sires
burn - ing
To hold you and to
fold you So close, close to my heart!
The eve-ning falls, so
f
rall.
3
a tempo
p a tempo

rall.
come to — me–
Come like the sigh-ing
wind from the sea, And
rall.
a tempo
bright-ly, so
light-ly, We'll
dance on the shin-ing
sand.
p
All thro' the
a tempo
night
That's filled with
sheer de - light, Our lamp of
love
will
p
rall.
3
mf a tempo
ev-er be bright, And
so all thro'
life we will
walk hand in
hand.
rall.
mf a tempo

Let my song fill your heart
With its mel-o-dy oh so di-vine,
That thrills me like a dream
Of hap-pi-ness su-preme.
It's en-chant-ing, it's sub-lime!
Let my

song say the words That my lips are a -
fraid to say– Of the yearn - ing And of de-sires
8
burn - ing To hold you and to fold you So close to my heart.
rall.
rall.
a tempo

MINNELIED

Felix Mendelssohn

sf
dolce
Tan - nen weit - hin grei - fen, und die Lin - de, und die
bank and bright the riv - er, And the lin - den, and the
p
Lin - de Blü - then streut!
lin - den strews her flow'rs.
pp
sf
sf
p
sf
p
In der Lin - de süss Ge - düf - te, in der Tan - nen Rie - sel -
Where the snow - y haw-thorn blanch-es, Where the woods so soft - ly
laut, in dem Spiel der Som-mer - lüf - te glän - zet sie als Frühlings -
sing, Where warm breez - es woo the branches, Shines my love, the bride of
p

p
cresc.
braut.
A - ber Wald - ton, Vo - gel - sin - gen, Duft der
Spring.
But ye fair and fragrant for - ests, And ye
p
cresc.
f
p cresc.
sf
Blü - then, hal - tet ein, Licht, ver - dunk - le, nie ge - lin - gen kann es
song - sters all, for - bear! Day - light, dark - en! ye can nev - er, ye can
f
p cresc.
p
f espress.
euch, kann es euch, ihr gleich zu sein! Nie ge - lin - gen
nev - er Be so bright, or sweet, or fair, ye can nev - er
p
pp
sf
kann es euch, ihr gleich zu sein!
be so bright, or sweet, or fair!
p
dim.

LET US DANCE, LET US SING

from "Dioclesian"

Henry Purcell

Let us revel, let us revel and play, let us, let us
revel and play, And rejoice
whilst we may, Since old Time, since old
Time these delights will remove.
colla voce

LIED DER MIGNON
(Mignon's Song)

Franz Schubert

Andante.
pp legato.
cresc.
pp
Ye who have yearned a-lone My grief can meas-ure, Ye who have yearned a-lone
Nur wer die Sehn-sucht kennt, weiss, was_ich lei - de, nur wer die Sehn-sucht kennt,
pp
My grief can meas-ure! No friends are near and flown Are joy_and
weiss, was_ich lei - de! Al-lein und ab-ge-trennt von al-ler
pp
dolciss.
pleas-ure; In yon-der sky I see But one_di-rec-tion, He's far, who
Freu-de, seh' ich an's Fir-ma-ment nach je-ner_Sei-te. Ach! der mich
ppp
dim.
gave to me His_heart's af-fec-tion. I'm
liebt und kennt, ist_in_der Wei-te. a tempo. Es
dim.

faint, and feel As though my heart were burn-ing, I'm
schwin-delt mir, es brennt mein Ein-ge-wei-de, es
cresc.
f
faint, and feel As though my heart were
schwin-delt mir, es brennt mein Ein - ge-
decresc.
p
burn - ing. Ye who have
wei - de. Nur wer die
decresc.
pp
yearned a - lone My grief can meas-ure, Ye who have yearned a-lone
Sehn - sucht kennt, weiss, was ich lei - de, nur wer die Sehn-sucht kennt,
sf
f
pp
My grief can meas - ure.
weiss, was ich lei - de!
p
cresc.
pp

A LITTLE CHINA FIGURE

Ethel Lindsay

Franco Leoni

pret - ty lit - tle house-maid came, And soft - ly dust - ed him.
She took him up so gen - tly, And with
such a charm-ing air,
His chi - na soul was melt - ed quite And
loved her to de - spair.
All day he sat and thought of her, Un -
f
p

til the twi - light came, And in his chi - na dreams at night He
breathed her lit - tle name. Ah! her lit - tle name,
her name, And in his chi - na dreams at night He
breathed her lit - tle name.
gliss.
cresc.

cresc.
f
dim.
mp
One day, while be - ing dust - ed, In his
p
joy he trem - bled so
To feel her lit - tle fin - gers, that A -
las! she let him go.
f
mf
In vain she tried to grab him back, Fate
mf

willed it they should part: He fell a-gainst the fen - der-edge And
broke his lit - tle heart.
f
She gath - ered up his frag - ments And she told a lit - tle
f
lie, Ex-pound - ing to her mis - tress how The cat had made him

die. And on the fol-low-ing morn-ing, when The shut-ters back she
thrust, She spoke his lit-tle ep-i-taph: "There's one thing less to
dust. Ah! there's one thing less, one thing
less to dust."
f
ten.
colla voce
p
gliss.
ff

LITTLE ELEGY

Elinor Wylie*

John Duke

*Reprinted from "The Collected Poems of Elinor Wylie" by permission of Alfred A. Knopf, Inc. Copyright, 1932, by Alfred A. Knopf, Inc.

pp
cresc.
mf
p
No bird have grace Or pow'r to sing; Or an - y-
thing ______ Be kind, or fair, And you
no - where.
pp
cresc.
mf
p
pp
pp
p
pp
mf
pp

LOVE HAS EYES

Charles Dibdin

Sir Henry Bishop
(1776-1855)

dolce e cantabile
But eyes a - lone the heart, In one soft look what lan-guage
lies, Oh, yes, be - lieve me, love has eyes, Oh, love has eyes,
riten.
col canto
a tempo
Love has eyes, Oh, love has eyes, Oh, yes, be-lieve me, love has eyes,
pp
con anima
cresc.
poco allarg.
Oh, yes, be-lieve me, Oh, yes, be-lieve me, Oh, yes, be-lieve me, love has
cresc.
col canto

eyes.
a tempo
leggero
sf
sf
p scherzando
2. Love's wing'd, they cry, Oh! nev - er! I, No pin - ions
pp
sempre stacc.
have to soar; De - ceiv - ers rove, But nev - er love,
p
cresc.
pp
cresc.
f
At - tach'd, he roves no more: Can he have wings who nev - er
dolce cantabile
f
p

riten.
flies? And yet, be - lieve me, Love has eyes, Oh, Love has eyes,
col canto
p a tempo
Love has eyes, Oh, Love has eyes, Oh, yes be - lieve me, Love has eyes,
pp stacc.
con anima
cresc.
f
poco allarg.
Oh, yes, be - lieve me, Oh, yes, be - lieve me, Oh, yes, be - lieve me, Love has
cresc.
f
col canto
eyes
a tempo
leggero
sf sf

LULLABY

Christina Rossetti

Cyril Scott

Allegretto grazioso
pp

p
Lul - - la - by, oh Lul - - la -

by, Flow'rs are closed and lambs — are —

sleep - - - ing, Lul - - la -
by, Lul - - la - by,
While the birds are si - lence_ keep - - - -
ing,_ Lul - - la - by, Oh
mf

Lul - - la - by, Sleep my
ba - by, fall a - sleep - - - ing
rit.
dim.
rit.
Lul - - la - by,
ritard.
p ritard.
Oh,
p
rit. - - - -
a tempo
Lul - - la - by,
Lul - - la -

by,
Oh,
Lul - - la -
by,
poco rit.
a tempo
Lul - - la - by,
poco rit.
a tempo
tranquillo
a tempo
tranquillo
pp
Lul - la - by,
Lul - la -
p
p
pp
a tempo
by,
rall.
pp

THE MERMAID'S SONG

Franz Joseph Haydn

Now the danc - ing sun - beams play
Come, be - hold what trea - sures lie
pp
On the green and glass - y sea.
Far be - low the roll - ing waves;
Come, and I will lead the way,
Rich - es hid from hu - man eye,
Where the
Dim ly
p
pearl - y trea - sures be,
shine in o - cean's caves.
cresc.

Come and I will lead the way, Where the pearl - y trea - sures be, Where the pearl - y trea - sures be, Where the pearl - y trea - sures be.
Eb - bing tides bear no de - lay, Storm - y winds are far a - way, Storm - y winds are far a - way, Storm - y winds are far a - way.
p
cresc.
cresc.
dim.
cresc.

Come with me, and we will go
f
where the rocks of co - ral grow, of co - ral grow,
p
Fol - low,
p
p
fol - low, fol - low me,
f
Fol - low, fol - low, fol - low
f
me.
Come with
3
leggieramente
3

me, and we will go where_ the_ rocks of co - ral_
p
grow, Where_ the_ rocks of co - ral_ grow, Fol - low,
f
fz
p
fol - low, fol - low me, Fol - low, fol - low, fol - low
f
me.
sf
sf
3
ff

NIGHT IS FALLING

based on the "Serenade" from the String Quartet Op. 3, No. 5

Franz Joseph Haydn
arranged by
Pauline Viardot-Garcia

English text by Willis Wager
French and Italian texts by Louis Pomey

spar - kling eyes of love? Ah, be - hold, 'tis the hour
clairs de tes beaux yeux! La voi - ci l'heure a - mou - reu -
sc'au - re a re - spi - rar. Non sà dir che sia di - let -
cre - - - scen - - - - do
Of mag - ic pow - er; All in flow - er Bids thee come and join our
se, Où, lan - gou - reu - se, L'â - me heu - reu - se S'a - ban - don - ne a cette ex -
- to, sia di - let - to, chi non po - sa in que - ste a - re - ne, chi non
play - ing, Cease de - lay - ing. The la - goon is now for -
ta - se Qui l'em - bra - se! La la - gune est so - li -
po - sa in que - ste a - re - ne. Or che len - to zef - fi -
sak - en As I glide a - long to thee; Come, my
tai - re; Sous les murs de ton pa - lais Glis - se ma
ret - to Dol - ce - men - te in - cre - spa il mar, or che

love, soft - ly wak - en While the breez - es fol - low
bar - que lé - gè - re Que ba - lance un air pur et
len - to zef - fi - ret - to Dol - ce - men - te in - cre - spa il
Ped.
p
free. I do call thee, I im - plore thee; When thou
frais. Je t'ap - pel - le! je t'im - plo - re! Quel - le
mar; Ma tu tre - mi, mio te - so - ro, ma tu
colla voce
pp
know - est I a - dore thee, What a - larm can bring thee
crain - te peut en - co - re, T'ar - rê - ter quand je suis
tre - mi, o mio te - so - ro, nè d'a - mor ti par - le -
fear? Come, my
là? Hâ - te -
rò? Ma tu

love, and has - ten light - ly, Nev - er mo - ment smiled more
toi, belle in - do - len - te, Ja - mais heu - re plus char -
pal - pi - ti cor' mi - o, non te - mer con te son
bright - ly On our love with bliss - ful cheer, with bliss - ful
man - te A l'a - mour ne sou - ri - ra, ne sou - ri -
i - o nè d'a - mor ti par - le - rò, ti par - le -
p
cheer, ah, bliss-ful cheer. All too soon will come the
ra, ne sou - ri - ra. Un ins - tant peut fai - re
rò, par - le - rò. Quan - do not - te il ciel im -
mor - row, All too soon from thee I must fly; Shall I
naî - tre Un obs - ta - cle à tant de bon - heur! Dois - je
bru - ni, Ni - ce in - gra - ta io ,par - ti - rò, Quan - do
Ped. pp
Ped. pp

then implore in sorrow, Ah, beloved, and grieving thus
donc sous ta fenêtre, O cruelle, mourir de dou-
not - te il ciel imbruni, Nice ingrata io parti-
die, Ah, beloved, ah, be-
leur! O cruelle! ô cru-
rò? Nice ingrata, Nice in-
rit.
rit. molto
loved, and grieving thus die, and grieving thus die, and grieving thus
elle! mourir de douleur, mourir de douleur, mourir de dou-
grata, io partirò, io partirò, io parti-
rit. molto
colla voce
a tempo
die?
leur!
rò?
a tempo
pp un poco accelerando
ppp

MY JOHANN
(Norwegian Dance)

Edvard Grieg
adapted by
Alexander Aslanoff

Adele Epstein

Allegretto tranquillo e grazioso
mf
Tra, la, la, la, la, la, la, la, la, la, When
mf

I go out to dance, my Jo-hann meets me. Oh! See what he's brought!

Oh! See what he's brought! Jo-hann's brought me flow-ers, Tra, la, la, la, la, la, la, la,

rall.
a tempo
Jo-hann's brought me flow-ers, Tra, la, la, la, la. Tra, la, la, la, la, la, la,
rall.
a tempo
la, la, la, And with a kiss the naugh-ty boy would greet me. Oh!
Should we be caught, Oh! Should we be caught, We would both catch ours,
Tra, la, la, la, la, la, la, la, We would both catch ours, Tra, la, la, la, la!

Allegro
f
Heigh! ho! thus! so! To and fro, 'round we go!
f staccato

p
Tra, la, la, la, la, la, la
p

Tra, la, la, la, la, la, la
leggero

f
tr
Ah
To and fro, 'round we go!
f

p
Tra, la, la, la, la, la, la
p

accelerando
Tra, la, la, la, la, la, la
cresc. ed accelerando

Tempo I°
p
Tra, la, la, la, la, la, la, la, la, la I al-ways have a lot of fun with Jo - hann.
marcato
p
Oh! I say him nay, But oh! He gets his way! I
sim - ply can't re - sist him, Tra, la, la, la, la, la, la, I
sim-ply can't re-sist him, Tra, la, la, la, la,
rall.
mf a tempo
Tra, la, la, la, la, la, la,
rall.
mf

la, la, la, I'm real-ly well be-haved you know, and so on,
So you will a-gree, Oh the fault's not with me,
If I real-ly kissed him, Tra, la, la, la, la, la, la, la, And I real-ly kissed him,
a poco
p
a poco
a poco rall. e dim.
Tra, la, la, la, la Ah!
pp
a poco rall. e dim.

O PEACE, THOU FAIREST CHILD OF HEAVEN

from the masque "Alfred"
by James Thomson and Davis Mallet

Thomas Arne
arranged by Guy Warrack

If the opening instrumental bars are found too long, a cut may be made from ✡ to ⌖

fair - est child of heav'n, To whom the syl - van
scene — was giv - en; The vale, the foun-tain
and the grove With ev' - ry soft - - - - - -
- - - - - - er, soft - er scene of love.
p
mf

p
Re - turn, sweet
Peace, and cheer the weep - ing swain, Re - turn, sweet
Peace, and cheer the weep-ing swain.
Re -
p
mf
pp
pp
pp
tr
3

p
turn with Ease and Plea-sure,
Re -
p
pp
tr
turn with Ease and Plea-sure.
mf
Re -
p
tr
pp
mf
pp
turn, re - turn
p
with
tr
3
pp
p

Ease and Plea - - - - - - - - - - -
- - - - - - - - - - - - - - - sure,
pp
with Ease and Plea - sure in thy train.
mf
pp
tr
3

SI MES VERS AVAIENT DES AILES!
(Were My Song With Wings Provided)

Reynaldo Hahn

vaient des ai - les Com - - me l'oi-
wings pro-vid - ed, Like to a
dim.
poco meno lento.
seau! Ils vo-le-raient, é - tin-
bird! Un-to the air so con-
cel - - les, Vers vo-tre foy-er qui
fid - - ed, Would thy chamber be its
rit Si mes vers a - vaient des ai - les
goal, Were my song with wings pro - vid - ed,
dim.

poco ritenuto.
pp
Com - me l'es-prit.
Like to the soul.
Tempo.
più lento, ritard. sin' al fine.
pp
Près de vous, purs et fi - dè - - les, Ils accourraient, nuit et
To thy heart a-non 'twere guid - - ed, As to her nest flies a
pp
p
jour
dove,
molto ritenuto.
Si mes vers a - vaient des ai - les,
Were my song with wings pro - vid - ed,
colla voce.
ancor più lento.
lunga.
pp
Si mes vers a - vaient des ai - les
were my song with wings pro - vid - ed,
Lento.
ppp
Com- me l'a - mour!
Like un-to love!
p
pp
ppp

OH, WHAT A BEAUTIFUL CITY!

African American spiritual
arranged by Edward Boatner

Oh, what a beau-ti-ful city! Twelve gates a-to de city, a-Hal-le - luh!
Three gates in_ a- de east, Three gates in_ a- de west, Three gates in_ a - de north,
Three gates in a- de south, Makin' it twelve gates a-to de city, a-Hal-le - luh!
Oh, what a beau-ti-ful city! Oh, what a beau-ti-ful city!

Oh, what a beau-ti-ful city! Twelve gates a-to de city, a-Hal-le-luh!
mf
My Lord built a-dat city, And He said it was just a-four square, And He
mf
f
said He want-ed you sinners To meet Him in a-de air, 'case He built
f

mf
Twelve gates a - to de city, a-Hal- le - luh.
f
Oh, what a beau-ti-ful city!
mf
p
f

Oh, what a beau - ti - ful city!
p
Oh, what a beau - ti - ful city!
p

Twelve gates, twelve gates, Hal - le - luh!
3
3
3
3
8

PIERCING EYES

Franz Joseph Haydn

Why asks my fair one if I love!
fz
p
f
p
Why, why, why asks my fair one if I love! Those eyes so pierc - ing
mf
p
bright! Can ev' - ry doubt of that re - move and need no oth - er
light, and need no oth - er light, and need no oth - er
fz

light.
Those
f
p
eyes_ full well do know_ my heart and all_ its work - ings see.
fz fz fz fz
mf p
E'er since they play'd the conq' - ror's part.
f
And I_ no more_ was free, and I_ no more_was
p

free. E'er since they play'd the conq' - ror's part.
And I no more was
free, and I no more was free, and
I no more was free, and I no more was free.
p
f
mf
f

ROSE SOFTLY BLOOMING

from *Azor'* and *Zemira*

Louis Spohr

Larghetto
p dolce
p
Rose soft - ly bloom - ing, Form'd to al - lure,
p
mf
Em - blem of Na - ture, Love - ly and pure!
p
mf
Em - blem of Na - ture, Love - ly and pure!
p

Thorns press a - round thee, Yet, gen - tle flow'r,
Smiles still are thine, The charm of the bow'r, The
Ossia
charm, the charm of the bow'r!
Nur - tured of Heav'n! Thy beau - ties I'll wear;
p
mf
p
mf

Pride of my bos - om! I'll cher - ish thee there:
p
mf
Pride of my bos - om! I'll cher - ish thee there:
p
p
mf
Un poco più vivace
Smiles still are thine, In the day's wast - ing hour;
mf
dim.
mf
dim.
So, gen - tle flow - er, So, gen - tle flow - er,
mf
dim.
mf
dim.

Tempo I
pp
Peace - ful - ly smil - ing, Oh, let me be,
pp
Ossia
dy - - ing, Sweet rose, sweet rose, like
Liv - ing and dy - - - ing, Sweet rose, like
colla parte
thee! Liv - ing and dy - ing, Sweet rose, like
p
p
mf
thee!
dim.

WALDEINSAMKEIT
(The Quiet of the Woods)

Max Reger

Con moto placido

sempre espressivo

p

Si - lent dusk lay o'er the
Ge - stern A - bend in der

sempre espressivo

p

p

col Pedale

sempre ben legato

leaf - y glade, Where, late, I watch'd a bird that
stil - len Ruh' sah ich im Wald ei - ner

home - - ward stray'd. While I lin-ger'd there,
Am - sel zu; als ich da so sass,

cresc. poco a poco

p

cresc. poco a poco

I - dle, un-a - ware, Comes my
mei - ner ganz ver - gass: kommt mein
sweet - heart, and steals a-round a lin-den tree, And
Schatz und schlei - chet sich um mich und
meno p
molto espressivo
poco rit
kiss - - - - es me!
küs - - - - set mich.
poco rit

(a tempo)
sempre espressivo
p
Leaves a man - y on the
So viel Laub als an der
a tempo
sempre espressivo
p
lin - - den be, Yet full as man - - y
Lin - - den ist und so viel tau - - send -
p
cresc. poco a poco
kiss - es had my love___ for me; For, I own, 'tis
mal hat mich mein Schatz___ ge - küsst; denn ich muss ge -
dim.
p
cresc. poco a poco

true,
steh'n,
For,
denn
I own, 'tis true, No one
ich muss ge - steh'n, es hat's
saw, — no — one knew, Save the hom - ing bird, and what be - fell,
nie - mand ge - seh'n, und die Am - sel soll mein Zeu-ge sein:
molto espressivo
rit.
He ne'er will tell!
wir war'n al - lein.

WATER PARTED FROM THE SEA

from "Artaxerxes"
translated from Metastastio

Thomas Arne

Though in search of lost re-
pose Through the land 'tis free to roam,
Still it mur-murs as it flows, Pant - ing for its na - tive home;

Though in search of lost — re - pose —
Through the land 'tis
free — to roam,
Still it — mur - murs as — it — flows,
Pant - ing for its na - tive home.

WHEN I HAVE SUNG MY SONGS

words and music by
Ernest Charles

Calmly ♩= 60

mp

rit.

mf

When I have sung my songs to you,— I'll sing no more. 'Twould be a sac-ri-lege

a tempo

mf

ten.
to sing— At an-oth-er door.
We've worked so hard
to hold our dreams,
espr.

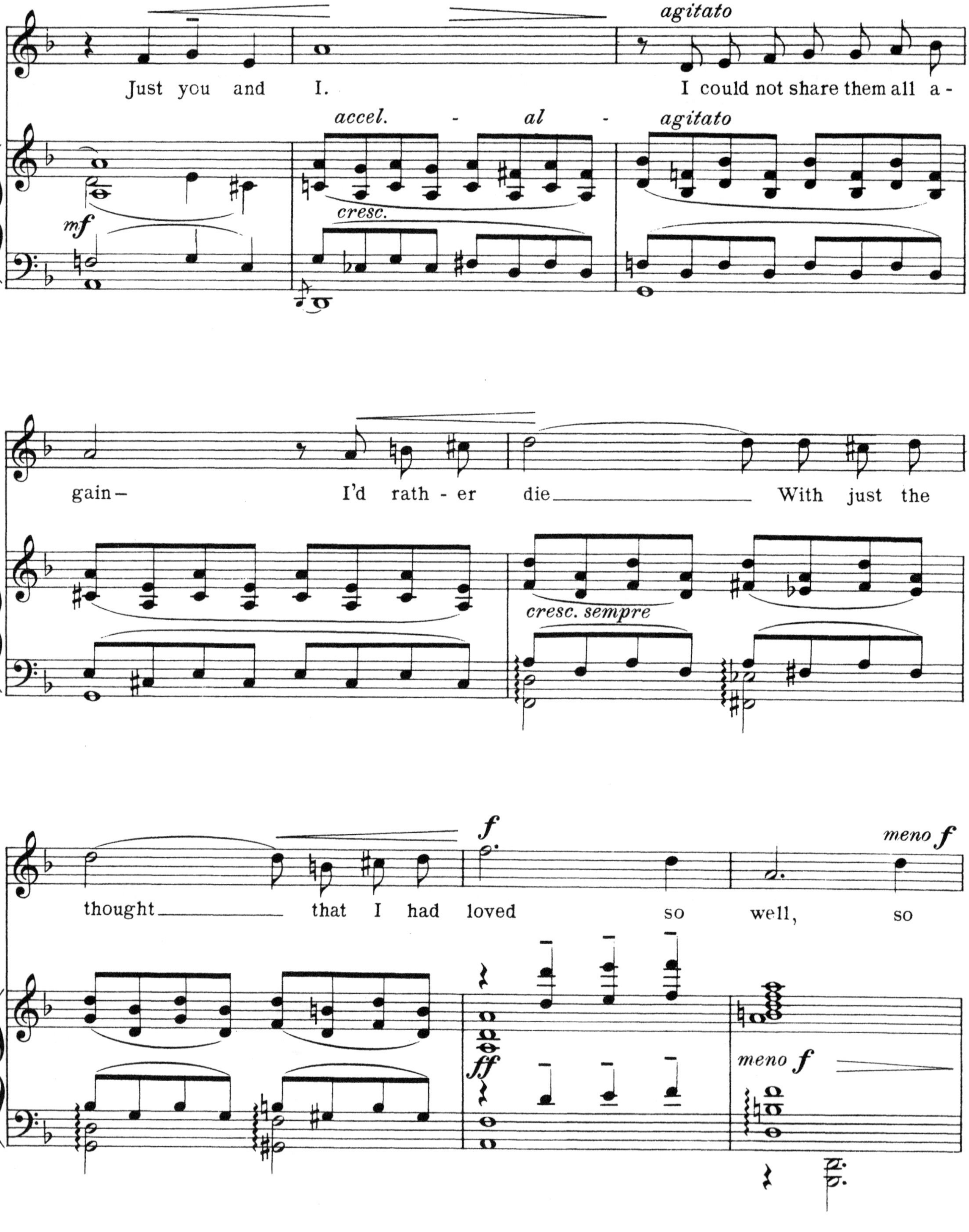

agitato
Just you and I. I could not share them all a -
accel. - al - agitato
mf
cresc.

gain– I'd rath - er die ——— With just the
cresc. sempre

f agitato
true, That I could nev - er sing a - gain,
mf
f
ff
That I could nev - er, nev - er sing a - gain, Ex - cept to
ff
dim.
you.
ten.
mf
rit.
p

THE FIRST BOOK OF SOPRANO SOLOS

PART II

PREFACE

The widespread acceptance by teachers and students of "The First Book Series" for Soprano, Mezzo-Soprano/Alto, Tenor, Baritone/Bass has prompted the development of a Part II addition for each voice type. After discussions with numerous voice teachers, the key suggestion expressed many times was that there is a need for "more of the same" type of literature at exactly the same level.

The volumes in Part II follow many of the same concepts which are covered in the Preface of the original volumes, including a comprehensive selection of between 34 and 37 songs from the Baroque through the 20th Century. The selections range from easy to moderate difficulty for both singer and accompanist.

In response to many requests, we have included more sacred songs, and have added two Christmas solos in each volume. The recommendation for more humorous songs for each voice was honored as well.

Even though these books have a heavy concentration of English and American songs, we have also expanded the number of Italian, German, and French offerings. For those using the English singing translations, we have tried to find the translations that are most singable, and in several cases have reworked the texts.

Part II can easily stand alone as a first book for a beginning high school, college, or adult student. Because of the varied contents, Part II can also be successfully used in combination with the first volume of the series for an individual singer. This will give many choices of vocal literature, allowing for individual differences in student personality, maturity, and musical development.

Hal Leonard Publishing (distributor of G. Schirmer) and Richard Walters, supervising editor, have been most generous in allowing the initial objective for this series to be expanded more fully through publishing these companion volumes. We hope this new set of books will provide yet another interesting and exciting new source of repertoire for both the teacher and student.

Joan Frey Boytim
September, 1993

About the Compiler...

Since 1968, Joan Frey Boytim has owned and operated a full-time voice studio in Carlisle, Pennsylvania, where she has specialized in developing a serious and comprehensive curriculum and approach to teaching and coaching adolescent and community adult students. Her teaching experience has also included music and choral instruction at the junior high and senior high levels, and voice instruction at the college level. She is the author of a widely used bibliography, *Solo Vocal Repertoire for Young Singers* (a publication of NATS), and, as a nationally recognized expert on teaching beginning vocal study, has been featured in many speaking engagements and presentations on the subject.

CONTENTS

ANIMAL CRACKERS

Christopher Morley

Richard Hageman

* From "Songs for a Little House", Copyright, 1917, by George H. Doran Company.

Meno mosso
think I shall al-ways in - sist up-on these. What do you choose when you're
, riten.
of-fered a treat? When Moth - er says, "What would you like best to eat?" Is it
riten.
questioningly
rall. poco
, with decision
Tempo I°
waf-fles and syr-up, or cin-na-mon toast? It's co-coa and an - i - mals
rall. poco

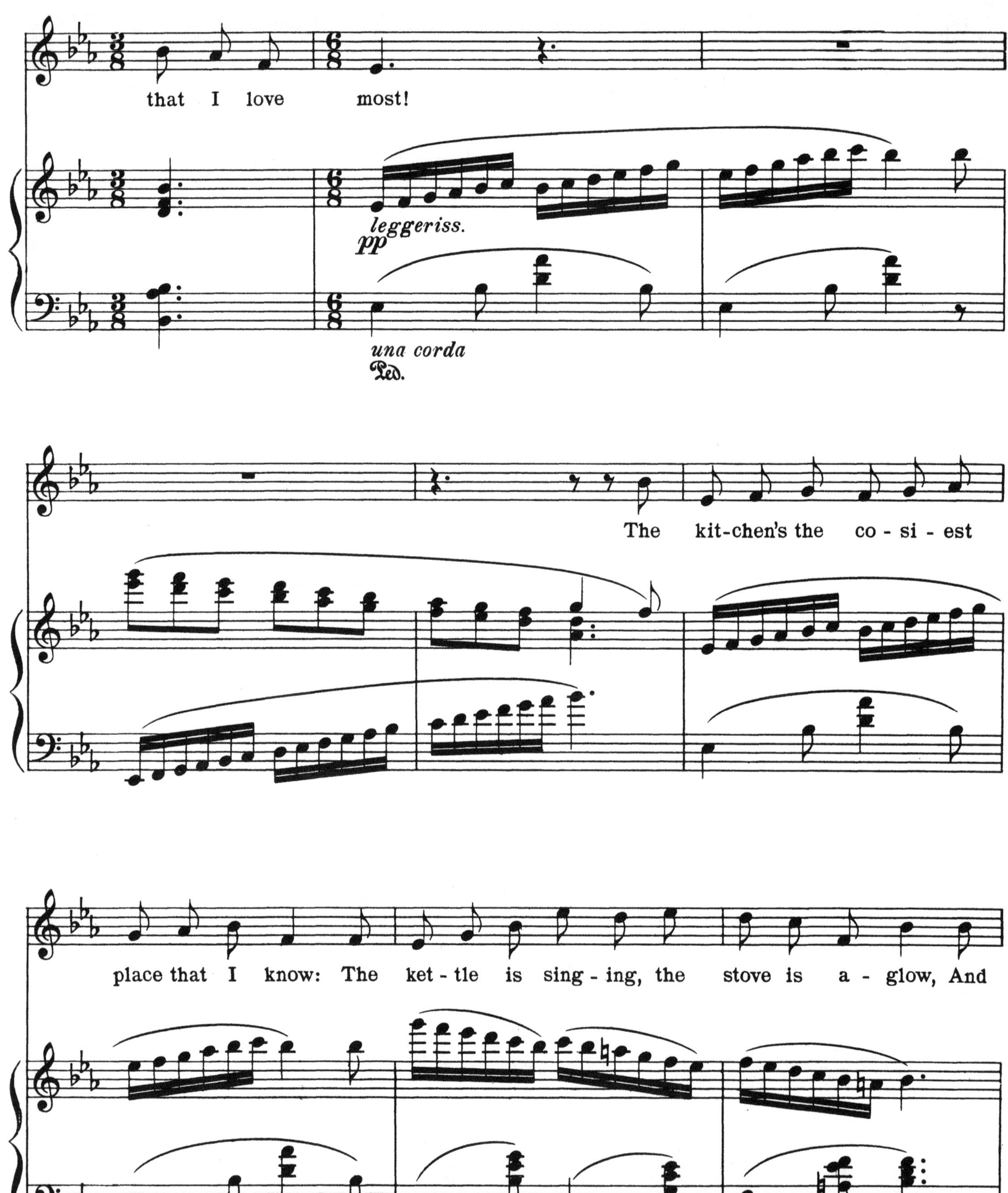
that I love most!
leggeriss.
pp
una corda
Ped.
The kit-chen's the co - si - est
place that I know: The ket - tle is sing - ing, the stove is a - glow, And

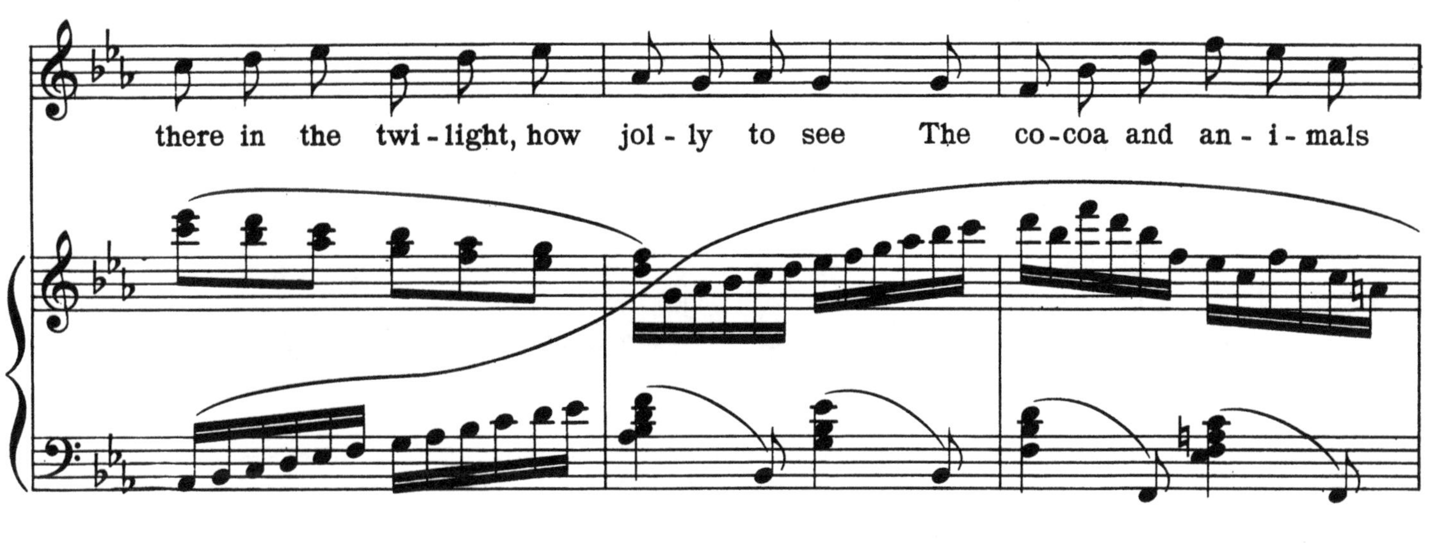
there in the twi-light, how jol-ly to see The co-coa and an-i-mals

wait-ing for me. Dad-dy and Moth-er dine lat-er in state, With
p
tre corde

Ma-ry to cook for them, Su-san to wait; But they don't have near-ly as
mf

much fun as I, Who eat in the kit-chen with Nurse stand-ing by; And
Lento
Tempo I°
Dad-dy once said, he would like to be me, Hav-ing co-coa and an-i-mals
f
once more for tea!
f
p
pp

COME AND TRIP IT

(from *L'Allegro*)

George Frideric Handel,
arranged by Mary Carmichael

Printed in the USA by G. Schirmer, Inc.

mf
Come and trip it as you go, On the light fan-
tas-tick. toe,
p
trip it, trip it,
mf
Come and trip it
as you go, as
cresc.
you go On the light fan-tas-tick toe.
f

p
Come and trip — it as — you go.
p
mf
Come and trip — it as — you go
f
mf
mf
On the light fan - tas - tick toe, trip it, trip it,
mf
mf
p
Come — and trip it as — you go,
p

p
cresc.
as
you go
p
cresc.
f
On the light fan - tas - tick toe.
f
f
f
p
Come and trip it as you go,
p
poco cresc.
trip it, trip it, trip it, trip it,
poco cresc.

f
On the light fan - tas - tick toe,
cresc.
Come, come, come, come and trip it
mf
as you go
allargando
On the light fan - tas - tick toe,
a tempo
On the light fan - tas - tick toe.

ANDENKEN

(I Think of Thee)

Friedrich von Matthison

Ludwig van Beethoven

Published in 1810.

Andante con moto.
tr
dolce
cresc.
sf

I think of thee ___ when thro' the grove the night - in gale's love ly
Ich den - ke dein, ___ wenn durch den Hain der Nach - ti - gal - len Ak -
p
cresc.

notes ___ are ring - ing; I think of thee! When, _
kor - de schal - len! Wann denkst du mein? wann, _
sf
p
sf

think'st thou of me? I think of thee in twi-light hours, Mid
wann denkst du mein? Ich den - ke dein im Dämmerschein der
p cresc.
p
jas - mine bowers And pass - ion - flowers! I think of
A - bend-hel-le am Schat - ten - quel-le! Wo denkst du
cresc.
sf
p
cresc.
thee; When thinkst thou of me? I think of thee a -
mein? wo, wo denkst du mein? Ich den - ke dein mit
sf
p cresc.
p
gain, a gain, With ar-dent yearning And love tears burning! Dost
sü-sser Pein, mit bangem Sehnen und hei - ssen Thränen! Wie
cresc.
sf
p

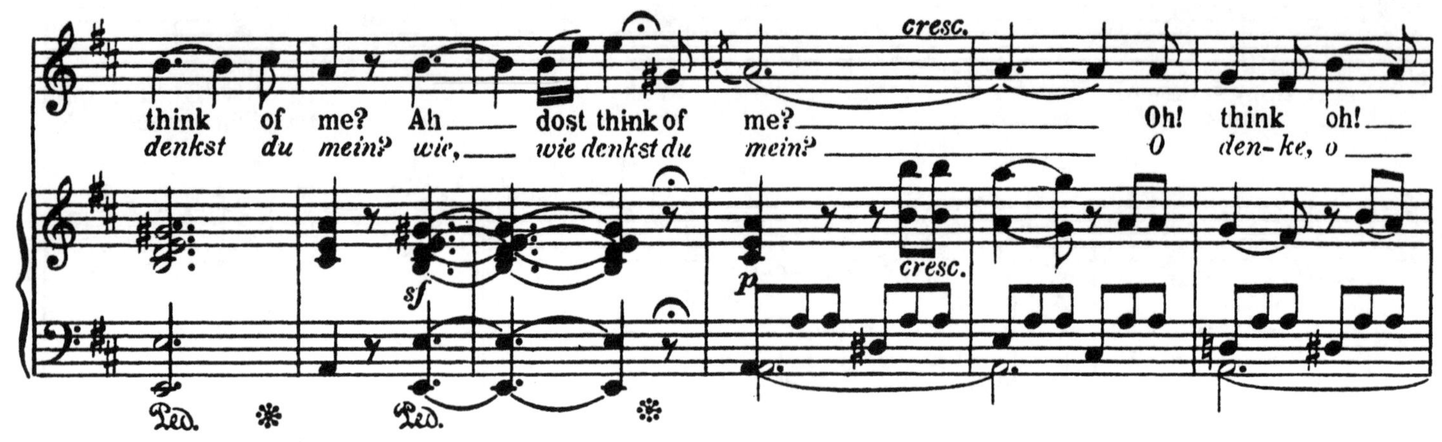
cresc.
think of me? Ah dost think of me? Oh! think oh!
denkst du mein? wie, wie denkst du mein? O den-ke, o
sf
p
cresc.
Ped.
Ped.

più mosso
think of me! Oh! think of me and hope that we May be u-nit-ed And
den-ke mein, o den-ke mein, bis zum Ver-ein auf besserm Ster-ne! In
più mosso
cresc.
sf
sf
fp
Ped. Ped.

love re-qui-ted! Ah! think of me, As I of thee! Oh!
je-der Fer-ne denk' ich nur dein, denk' ich nur dein! O
f
p
Ped.

più mosso
dear-est, oh! think of me! Oh think of me and pray that
den-ke, o den - - ke mein, o den-ke mein, bis zum Ver-
più mosso
cresc.
we May be u-nit-ed And love-re-quit-ed! ah! think of me, as I of
ein auf bes-serm Ster-ne! In je-der Fer-ne denk' ich nur dein, denk' ich nur
sf
sf
fp
f
p
thee! Ah! think of me, As I of thee! For I am
dein, denk' ich nur dein, nur dein, nur dein, nur dein, nur
thine; I am thine, am thine!
dein! ja, nur dein, nur dein!
pp
p
sf
pp

AVE MARIA
(O Lord, Most Holy)

Franz Abt

Printed in the USA by G. Schirmer, Inc.

f
tu in mu - li - e - ri -
prais - ing with joy - ful
mf
bus, et be - ne -
lips: For Thou hast re -
di - ctus, be - ne - di - ctus
deem - ed us, Thou hast re -
p dim.
fru - ctus ven - tris tu - i
deem - ed us, by Thy grace and

pp
Je - sus.
mer - cy.
mf
p poco animato
San - cta Ma -
Teach us to
poco animato
p
ri - a, ma - ter
know Thee, Teach us to
Dè - i o - ra pro
love Thee, Make us to

no - bis, pro no - bis pec - ca -
fol - low, to fol - low af - ter
Tempo I
mf tranquillo
to - ri - bus: O - ra pro
ho - li - ness; So in temp -
Tempo I
poco rit.
p tranquillo
optional
ho - ra mor - tis
hour of our
no - bis, nunc et in ho - ra
ta - tion And in the hour of
no - strae
sad - ness
molto cresc.
mor - tis o - ra,
sad - ness We shall find

sf
dim.
o - ra pro no -
com - fort and help in
sf
dim.
bis.
Thee.
San - cta Ma -
Guide us O
p
Ped.
ri - a,
Sa - vior
o - ra pro
O lov - ing
no - bis
Sa - vior,
p
nunc et in ho - ra
So in the hour of

ho - ra mor - tis
hour of our
mf
mor - tis,
sad - ness
nunc et in ho - ra
We shall find com - fort and
mf
no - strae
sad - ness
mor - tis.
help in Thee.
A -
dim.
a tempo
p
f
rit.
men,
A -
p
p
f
rit.
pp
men.
p
dimin. al
pp
pp

CHARMANT PAPILLON

(Charming Butterfly)

English text by
Mrs. O. B. Boise

André Campra

Printed in the USA by G. Schirmer, Inc.

p leggiero
Charmant pa-pil-lon, dont l'ai-le d'or pas-se Dans l'es-pa-
Brilliant but-ter-fly, whose wings gai-ly glis-ten, Fair-est flow-
ce Comme u-ne fleur!
ers dost thou out-vie!
cresc.
Charmant pa-pil-lon, dont l'ai-le d'or pas-se Dans l'es-
Bril-liant but-ter-fly, whose wings gai-ly glis-ten, Fair-est
pa- ce Comme u-ne fleur! Que ne
flow- ers dost thou out-vie! Would that
mf

p
puis-je, sur ta tra - ce, M'en - vo - ler a - vec toi com -
I might be thy com - rade! Ah, how glad - ly I'd fol - - - low
p
me u - ne sœur!
thee for aye!
f
p
Char - mant pa - pil - lon, dont l'ai - le d'or pas - se Dans les
Bril - liant but - ter - fly, whose wings gai - ly glis - ten, Fair - est
p
p
pa - - - - - - ce Com - me u - ne
flow - - - - - - ers dost thou out -

p
fleur; Je vou - drais vo - ler a - vec
vie! I would glad - - - - ly, so glad-ly
p
poco rit.
toi com - me u - ne sœur!
fol - - - - - low thee for aye!
poco rit.
a tempo
f
p
poco rit.
p
C'est à pei - ne si tu te po - ses,
With - out rest thou art ev - er flit - ting,
f

mf
C'est à pei - ne si tu te po - ses
with - out rest thou art ev - er flit - ting,
mf
p
poco cresc.
Sur la feuil - le ten - dre des ro - ses, Dans l'es - pa - - -
From the bud - ding blush - ros - es sip - ping, Dost thou seek
p
poco cresc.
pp
- ce que tu par - cours. Ah!
in their hearts re - pose? Ah!
pp
cresc.
f rit.
pp a tempo
que tes bon jours Sont courts! Char - mant pa - pil - lon, dont l'ai - le d'or
too soon thy life must close! Bril - liant but - ter - fly, whose wings gai - ly
cresc.
f rit.
pp a tempo

pas - se Dans l'es - pa - - - - -
glis - ten, Fair - -est flow- - - - -
- - - - ce Com - me u - ne fleur! Je vou -
- - - - ers thou dost out - vie! I would
drais vo - ler a - vec toi
glad - - - ly, so glad - ly fol - - -
com - me u - ne sœur.
- - - - - low thee for aye.
p
cresc.
rit.
rit.
cresc.
rit.
rit.

COME TO THE FAIR

Helen Taylor

Easthope Martin

*The Introduction may be commenced at the sign ⌖

Printed in the USA by G. Schirmer, Inc.

f
mf
Heigh - ho! come to the fair! All the stalls on the green are as fine as can
f
mf
be With trinkets and tokens so pretty to see, So it's come then,
riten.
f a tempo
mf
maidens and men, To the fair in the pride of the morn - ing So deck yourselves
f
out in your finest ar - ray, With a heigh - ho!
ff
poco rit.

ten. ten. ten.
come to the fair!
allargando
col canto
f a tempo
mf
The fid-dles are play-ing the tune that you
mf
f
ff
know: "Heigh - ho! come to the fair!" The drums are all
ff
f
mf
beat-ing, a-way let us go, Heigh - ho! come to the fair! There'll be

rac-ing and chas-ing from morn-ing till night, And round-a-bouts turn-ing to
left and to right, So it's come then, maid-ens and men, To the fair in the
pride of the morn - ing, So lock up your house, there'll be plen-ty of fun, And it's
heigh - ho! Silence come to the fair!
riten.
a tempo
f a tempo
ritard.
attacca
ff a tempo
ten.

For love mak-ing too, if so be you've a mind, Heigh - ho! come to the fair! For hearts that are hap-py are lov-ing and kind,
Heigh - ho! come to the fair! If "Haste to the wed-ding" the fid-dles should play, I
war-rant you'll dance to the end of the day;— Come then, maid-ens and men To the

fair in the pride of the morn - ing The sun is a-shin-ing to wel-come the
mf
day, With a heigh - ho! come to the fair, Maid-ens and men,
f
maid-ens and men, Come to the fair in the morn - ing, Heigh -
poco ritard.
molto allargando
ten. ten.
ho come to the fair!
più ritard.
ff col canto
a tempo

THE CRYING OF WATER

Arthur Symons

Louis Campbell-Tipton

Moderato ma con passione
Voice
Piano
Voix des
Wa - - ter,
Eaux,
rit.
voice of my heart,
voix de mon cœur, Tu
mf a tempo
ff rall.
a tempo
cry - ing in the sand,
gé - mis sur le sa - ble,

mp
p
All night long cry - ing
Et la nuit s'é - meut
m.g.
m.g.
pp
with mourn - ful cry.
de ta dou - leur.
Dis -
fff
ff
mf
cresc.
As I lie and lis - ten, and
moi si ta cla - meur Et
f

can - not un - der - - stand The
ton cri la - men - - ta - ble
in light, flexible voice
voice of my heart in my side, or the voice of the sea.
ont jail - li de mon sein, ou de la mer en pleurs.
O wa - - - - - ter,
Ô flots,

ff
wa - - - - - - ter,
flots, Al - té -
ff
f
cry - ing for rest,
rés de re - pos,
f
ff
mp
pp
Is it I? is it I?
N'ê - tes-vous pas mon â - me en pei - ne?
mp

pp
All night
Voix des
mp
mp
m.g.
long
Eaux,
pp
The wa - ter is
Ta plain - te lu -
mp
pp
rall.
ppp
cry - - ing to me.
gu - - bre est la mienne.
rall. e dim.
pppp

HERE AMID THE SHADY WOODS

Thomas Morell

George Frideric Handel
(1685-1759)

Taste, my soul, this charm-ing seat, Love and glo - ry's calm re - treat.
tr
Here a - mid the sha - dy woods, —
Taste, my soul, this charm - ing seat, Love and glo - ry's calm re -
treat. —
Here a - mid the sha - dy woods, Fra - grant

flow'rs and crys-tal floods, Taste, my soul, this charming seat, Love and glo - ry's calm re -
treat, taste, my soul, this charm-ing seat, love and glo - ry's calm re - treat,
love and glo - - ry's calm re - treat.
mf

DRIFT DOWN, DRIFT DOWN

(Winter)

Harold Simpson

Landon Ronald

Printed in the USA by G. Schirmer, Inc.

molto rall.
a tempo
peace at last: Drift down, drift down from the skies,
a tempo
colla voce
Lit-tle white snow-flakes, fall - ing fast.
p
p
mf
Fall soft, fall soft on my love, Lit-tle white snow-flakes
mf

drift - ing down, Mes-sen-gers from the skies a - bove,
On the winds of pas - sion blown;
p
Fall soft, fall soft on my love, Lit-tle white snow-flakes
p f
drift - ing down.
f
8

p come primo
Drift down, drift down from the skies, Lit-tle white snow-flakes fall-ing fast,
p come primo
f
p
molto rall.
a tempo
Like sleep that falls on tired eyes To bring us peace at last: Drift down, drift down
f
p
molto rall.
a tempo
pp falsetto
mf
from the skies, Lit-tle white snow - flakes, Lit-tle white snow-flakes fall-ing
pp
mf
p
fast.
p
Ped.

GESÙ BAMBINO

(The Infant Jesus)

Frederick H. Martens

Pietro Yon

p
an - gels sang, the shep - herds sang, The grate - ful earth re - joiced,
f
And at His bless - ed birth the stars Their ex - ul - ta - tion
f
voiced. O come let us a -
Opt: Ve - ni - te a - do -
pp
Non troppo lento
pp

dore Him, O come let us a - dore Him, O
re - mus, Ve - ni - te a - do - re - mus, Ve -
rall.
come let us a - dore Him, Christ the
ni - te a - do - re - mus, Do - mi -
rall.
Lord.
num.
p
A -
Tempo I
gain the heart with rap - ture glows To greet the ho - ly night That
p

a tempo
rall.
gave the world its Christ - mas Rose, Its King of Love and Light. Let
rall.
a tempo
ev' - ry voice ac-claim His name, The grate - ful cho - rus swell,
From par - a - dise to earth He came That we with Him might
dwell.
O come let us a -
Ve - ni - te a - do -

dore Him, O come let us a - dore Him, O
re - mus, Ve-ni - te a - do - re - mus, Ve-
rall.
come let us a - dore Him Christ the
ni - te a - do - re - mus Do - mi-
rall.
Lord.
num.
p
Ah!
Ah!
O come let us a - dore Him, Ah!
Ve - ni - te a - do - re - mus Ah!

a - dore Him Christ the Lord. O
a-do-re - mus Do - mi-num. Ve -
come, O come,
ni - te, ve - ni - te,
O come let us a - dore Him, let us a -
ve-ni - te a - do - re - mus, a - do -
rall.
p a tempo
dore Him, Christ the Lord.
re - mus Do - mi-num.
pp a tempo
f rall.

GRANDMA

Leonard Feeney

Theodore Chanler

Grand-ma's hair Is white, And she loves to sit In her
p

rock-ing-chair, And knit And talk And al - most rock,

sempre p
And see you dim - ly with her poor eye - sight.

Grand-ma says That
cresc.
f
p

God Is good, But that His ways Are odd And can-not be

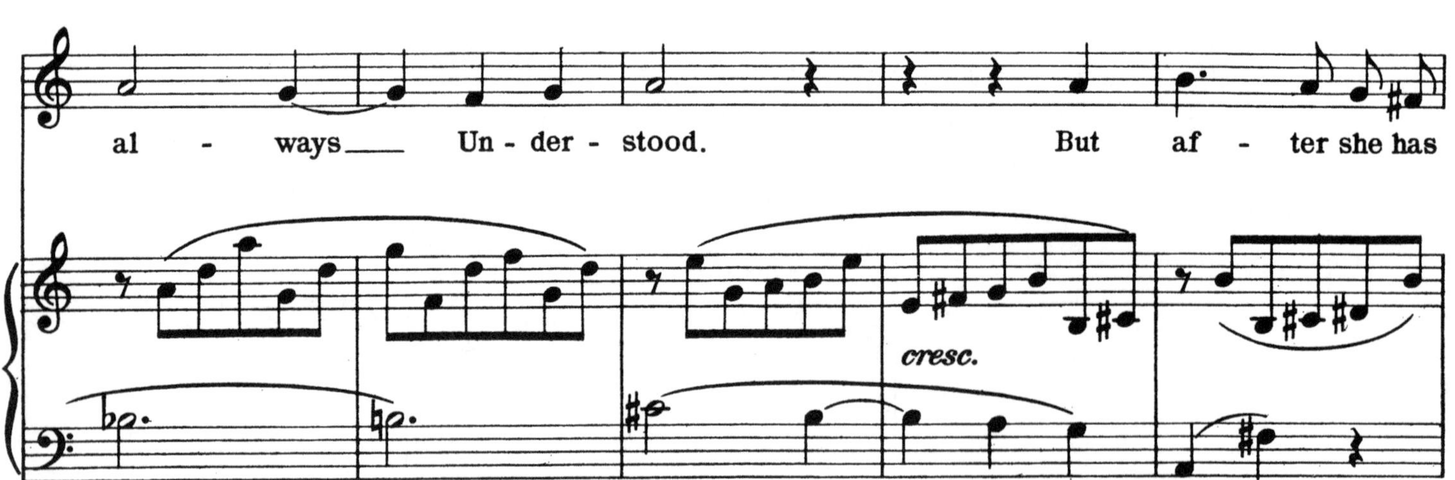
al - ways Un-der-stood. But af - ter she has
cresc.

tak - en a cook-ie from the shelf, And giv-en it to you And

p subito
smiled,
You know that she her-self Was
dim.
p

un poco rubato
once a lit-tle child, And had a grand-ma too.
rit.
dim.
pp

L'HEURE EXQUISE

(The Hour of Dreaming)

translation by Theodore Baker

Reynaldo Hahn

Tranquillo e dolce possibile
pp
p
La lu - ne blan - che Luit dans les bois;
The moon-beams whit - en Boughs all a - round,
De cha - que bran - che Part u - ne voix Sous la ra -
Wher-e'er they light - en Voic - es re - sound Dim in the
poco
sf
mé - e...
gloam - ing:
p

delicatamente
p
O bien - ai - mé - - - - - - - e!
Love, art thou com - - - - - - - ing?
pp
discreto
L'é - tang re - flè - te, Pro - fond mi - roir, La si - lhou -
A cloud - y mir - ror, Wa - ters be - low Dark - ly the
et - - - te Du sau - le noir Où le vent pleu - re... Rê -
pil - - - lar In out - line show, Where winds are weep - ing: Oh
vons! c'est l'heu - - - - - re...
love! art sleep - - - - - ing?
dim.

ancor più tranquillo
Un vaste et ten - dre A-pai - se - ment Sem - ble des -
A deep and ten - der Calm now lies O'er all things
ancor più p
pp
rallent.
cen-dre Du fir - ma - ment Que l'astre i - ri - se...
un-der Yon arch-ing skies Where stars are gleam - ing:
a tempo
colla voce
pp
C'est l'heu - re ex - qui - se.
Oh hour di - vine of dream - ing!
senza ritardare
pp
ppp

HOW LOVELY ARE THY DWELLINGS

Psalm 54

Samuel Liddle

Printed in the USA by G. Schirmer, Inc.

p
Yea, the spar - row hath found her a house, and the swal - low a
tranquillo
p
rit.
a tempo
nest, where she may lay her young, ev - en Thine al - tars,
rit.
a tempo
cresc
allargando
ev - en Thine al - tars, O Lord of Hosts, my
cresc
f allargando
King and my God.
a tempo
dim
poco rit.
p

p
O Lord God of Hosts, hear my prayer. I would
pp [Organ alone]
ra - ther be a door - keep-er in the house of my God, than to
cresc
dwell in the tents of wick - ed - ness .... For a
con fervore
f
day in Thy courts is bet - ter than a thou - sand. How
mf [Piano and Organ]
f

Tempo primo.
love - ly are Thy dwell - ings, O Lord of
Hosts! My soul long - eth yea faint - eth, for the
courts of the Lord: my heart and my flesh cry
out for the liv - - ing God
Ped.
mf
rit.
rit.

a tempo
p
Yea, the spar - row hath found her a house, and the swal - low a
a tempo
p
tranquillo
[Piano alone]
rit.
a tempo
cresc
nest, where she may lay her young, ev - en Thine al - tars,
[With Organ]
rit.
a tempo
cresc
cresc
allargando
rall.
f
ev - en Thine al - tars, O Lord of Hosts, my
allargando
cresc
rall.
King and my God.
rit.
colla voce
a tempo
dim
p
slow arpeggio.

ICH LIEBE DICH

(I Love You)

Poem by Herrosee
English by
Lorraine Noel Finley

Ludwig van Beethoven

Andante
Voice
Piano
p ben sostenuto
As you love me, so I love you, In fair or storm-y weath - er. We
Ich lie - be dich, so wie du mich, am A - bend und am Mor - gen, noch
share our lives each day a-new, And face our cares to - geth - er.
war kein Tag, wo du und ich nicht teil-ten un - sre Sor - gen;
mf
We saw our bur-dens' weight decrease With ev - 'ry dawn - ing mor - row; You
Auch wa - ren sie für dich und mich ge - teilt, leicht zu er - tra - gen, du
ben sostenuto
brought my aching heart surcease, My tears assuaged your sor-row, As - suaged your sor - row. And
trös - te-test im Kummer mich, ich weint' in dei - ne Kla-gen, in dei - ne Kla - gen, d'rum
f
dolce

cresc.
thus may God who reigns a-bove, And hears my heart con - fess - ing, Pro -
Got - tes Se - gen ü - ber dir, du mei - nes Le - bens Freu - de, Gott
p
cresc.
f
p
tect you, dear, with all His love, And grant us both His bless-ing, Pro -
schü - tze dich, er - halt' dich mir, schütz' und er - halt' uns Bei - de, Gott
f
p
cresc.
f
p
tect you, dear, with all His love, And grant us both His bless-ing, And
schü - tze dich, er - halt' dich mir, schütz' und er-halt' uns Bei - de, er -
cresc.
f
p
mf
f
mp
grant us both His bless-ing, And grant His bless - ing!
halt', er-halt' uns Bei - de, er - halt' uns Bei - de.
p
mf
f
mp
cresc.
f

INTORNO ALL'IDOL MIO

(Caressing Mine Idol's Pillow)

English version by
Theodore Baker

Marco Antonio Cesti

cresc.
rfz
più cresc.
let - te ba - cia - te - lo per me, cor - te - si, cor -
breez - es, In greet - ing bear from me, The sweet - est, the
Ped. *
rfz
p
poco rit.
te - si au - ret - - - te! e nel - le guan - cie e -
sweet-est of kiss - - - es! And to his cheek, kind
rfz
p smorz.
poco rit.
p
smorz.
cresc.
let - te ba - cia - te - lo per me, ba - cia - te - lo per me, cor -
breezes, In greet - ing bear from me, in greet - ing bear from me the
cresc.
rfz
p
rit.
tr
te - si, cor - te - si au - ret - - te!
sweet-est, the sweet-est of kiss - - es!
rfz
p
col canto pp

mf
cresc.
Al mio ben, che ri - po - sa su l'a - - li
To my love, who his spir - it to rest - ful
p
dim.
cresc.
rfz
del - la qui - e - te, gra - ti, gra - ti
night doth sur - ren - der, Waft ye, waft ye
poco rit.
p
so - gni as - si - ste - - te E il mio racchiu - so ar -
fair dreams and ten - - der, And all my pas - sion re -
più cresc.
do - re sve - la - te - gli per me, o lar - ve, o
press - ed Re - veal to him for me, O vis - ion, O
cresc.

rfz portando
pp
tr
mf
lar - ve d'a - mo - - re, e il
vis - ion so bless - - ed! And
rfz
p
mf
mio rac-chiu - so ar - do - re sve - la - te-gli per me, sve -
all my pas - sion re-press-ed Re - veal to him for me, re -
decresc.
cresc.
rfz
la - te-gli per me, o lar - ve, o lar - ve d'a -
veal to him for me, O vis - ion, O vis - ion so
cresc.
rit.
mo - - re!
bless - - ed!
p col canto
p
dim.
pp

LACHEN UND WEINEN
(Laughing and Crying)

Friedrich Rückert
translation by Joan Boytim

Franz Schubert

Etwas geschwind
pp
La - chen und Wei - nen zu jeg - li - cher Stun - de
Laugh - ing and cry - ing my heart has its sea - sons;
ruht bei der Lieb auf so man - cher - lei Grun - de.
Where is the cu - pid who knows all the rea - sons?

Printed in the USA by G. Schirmer, Inc.

Mor - gens lacht' ich vor Lust
Why I laughed at break of day,
und wa - rum ich nun
And why now I am
pp
decresc.
wei - - - ne bei des A - ben - des
weep - ing, cry - ing here in the
Schei - ne, ist mir selb' nicht be -
eve - ning glow? I my - self do not
a tempo
dim.
mf

wußt, ist mir selb' nicht be - wußt.
know, I my - self do not know.
pp
Wei - nen und
Cry - ing and

La - chen zu jeg - li - cher Stun - de ruht bei der
laugh - ing my heart has its sea - sons; Where is the
Lieb auf so man - cher - lei Grun - de.
cu - pid who knows all the rea - sons?
A - bends weint' ich vor Schmerz;
Why my tears at eve - ning fall,
und wa - rum du er - wach - en kannst am Mor - gen mit
and why in the morn - ing do I wake up with
cresc.

La - chen,
laugh - ter?
muß ich dich fra - - gen, o
It's on - ly you, O heart, can
f
Herz, muß ich dich fra - gen, o Herz.
tell, it's on - ly you, O heart, can tell.
pp

THE LAST ROSE OF SUMMER

Thomas Moore

Richard Alfred Miliken
Setting by Friedrich Von Flotow

Larghetto

p

'Tis the last rose of summer, Left bloom - ing a - lone. All her love - ly com - pan - ions are fa - ded and gone. No flow - er of her kin - dred, No rose - bud is nigh, To re -

Printed in the USA by G. Schirmer, Inc.

flect back her blush - es, Or give sigh for sigh!
f
I'll not leave thee, thou lone one, To
pine on the stem, Since the love - ly are sleep - ing, Go
sleep thou with them. Thus kind - ly I scat - ter Thy

leaves o'er the bed, Where thy mates of the
garden Lie scent - less and dead, Where thy
mates of the gar - den Lie scent - less and
dead.
cresc.
f
dim.

NO FLOWER THAT BLOWS

Thomas Linley

p
scat-ters such per-fume, or scat-ters such per-fume; No flow'r that
p
blows is like, is like this rose, no flow'r that blows is
like, is like this rose: Up-on my breast, ah! gen-tly
rest And ev-er, ev-er bloom, and ev-er, ev-er bloom.

p
No flow'r that blows is like, is like this rose,
p
no flow'r that blows is like, is like this rose, Dear
pledge to prove a pa - rent's love, A pleas - ing,
pleas - ing gift thou art; Come, sweet-est flow'r, and

f
from this hour Live hence-forth in my heart, live hence-forth in my
heart.
p
No flow'r that blows is like, is like this
rose, no flow'r that blows is like, is like this
rose.

A NUN TAKES THE VEIL

Gerard Manley Hopkins

Samuel Barber

poco f
And I have asked to be Where
l.h.
poco f
no storms come, Where the green swell is in the ha-vens dumb,
f
f
rall. molto
p
3
pp
And out of the swing of the sea.
p rall. molto
pp

NUR WER DIE SEHNSUCHT KENNT

(None But the Lonely Heart)

Johann Wolfgang von Goethe
Translated by Arthur Westbrook

Pyotr Il'yich Tchaikovsky

Printed in the USA by G. Schirmer, Inc.

part - ed far From joy and glad - ness.
ab - ge - trennt von al - - ler Freu - de.
p
p
Heav'n's bound - less
Seh' ich an's
un poco marcato
arch I see Spread out a - bove me.
Fir - ma - ment nach je - ner Sei - te.
mf
Ah! what a
Ach! der mich
cresc.
mf
dis - tance drear To one who loves me!
liebt und kennt ist in der Wei - te.
dim.
pp
pp

f
None but the lone - ly heart
Nur wer die Sehn - sucht kennt,
cresc.
mf
p
Can know my sad - ness;
weiss, was ich lei - de!
cresc.
A - lone, and
Al - lein und
p
cresc.
part - ed far From joy and glad - ness,
ab - ge - trennt von al - ler Freu - de,
f
cresc.
A - lone, and part - ed far
Al - lein und ab - ge - trennt
cresc. e string.

ff
pp molto rit.
From joy and glad - ness.
My sen - ses
von al - ler Freu del
Es schwin - delt
ff
molto rit.
a tempo
fail,
A burn - ing fire de -
mir,
es brennt mein Ein - ge -
p a tempo
vours me.
None but the lone - ly heart Can
wei - de,
Nur wer die Sehn - sucht kennt, weiss,
know my sad - ness.
was ich lei - del
pp

ORPHEUS WITH HIS LUTE

from *Henry VIII* by William Shakespeare

William Schuman

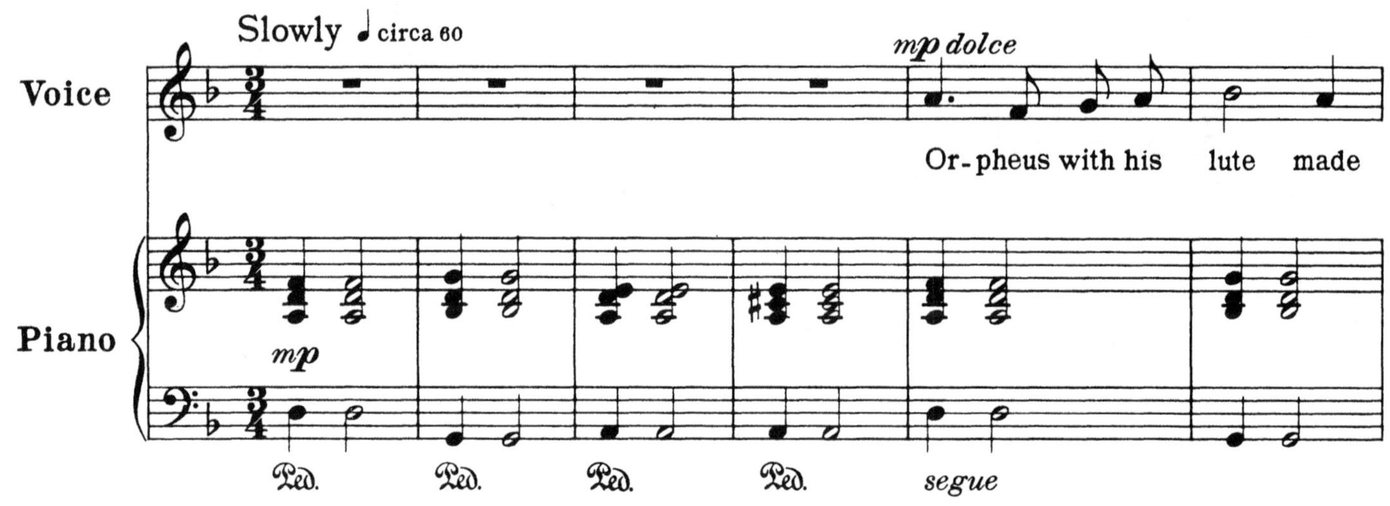

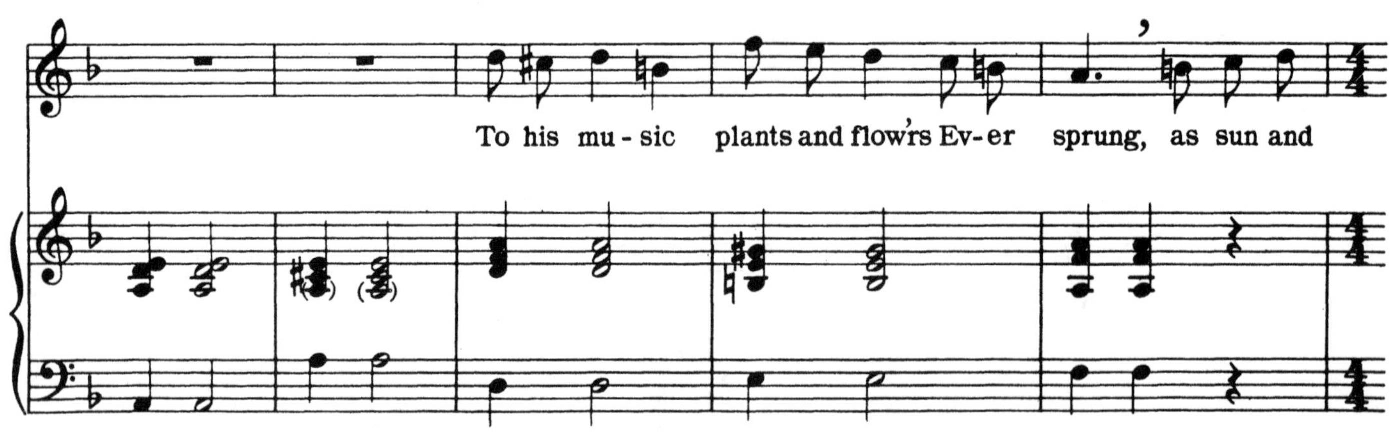

mf
show'rs There had made a last-ing spring.
Ev-'ry thing that heard him
play, E-ven the bil-lows of the sea,
mp
Hung their heads, and then lay
by.
p
In sweet mu-sic is such art, Kill-ing care and grief of
heart, Fall a-sleep, or hear-ing, die.

New Rochelle, N.Y.
August 6, 1944

O SAVIOUR, HEAR ME!

Dudley Buck

Christoph Willibald Gluck,
arranged by Dudley Buck

Andante.
VIOLIN. ad libit.
VOICE.
PIANO or ORGAN.
p
tranquillo.
1. O Sa - viour hear me, I im - plore thee,
2. When cares of earth to me seem hea - vy
In thee a - lone can peace be found,
Heart - sore I seek of thee re - lief,

Thou canst sus - tain and thou re - store me
Thy grace re - main - eth ev - - - er rea - dy
What - e'er the cares that hov - - er round.
To soothe my pain, to as - suage my grief.
p
Hear my sup - - pli - - ca - - tion.
8va ad lib.
Turn on me thy lov - - ing eyes, O

turn on me thy lov - - ing eyes;
Lord I long for thy sal - va - - tion,
And would fain at - - tain the
1. 2.
prize. prize,
rall.
pp

LA PASTORELLA

The Shepherd Maid

Carlo Goldoni
English text by
Lorraine Noel Finley

Franz Schubert

Printed in the USA by G. Schirmer, Inc.

tà, can - tan - do in li - ber - tà.
free, Her heart was fan - cy - free.
Se l'in - no-cen-te a-mo - re gra - di - sce il suo pa - sto - re, la
If shep - herd lad's de - jec - tion Re - veal his true af - fec - tion, With
fp
bel - la pa - sto - rel - la con - ten - ta o - gnor sa -
grow - ing ar - dor show - ing, How hap - py she will
fp
rà, con - ten - ta o - gnor sa - rà. La
be, How hap - py she will be! A
fp
p

pa - sto - rel - la al pra - to con - ten - ta se - ne
shep - herd maid sang bright - ly A song that filled the
va, coll' a - gnel - li - no a la - to can -
lea, While lambs were frol - ick - ing light - ly, Her
tan - do in li - ber - tà, can - tan - do in li - ber -
heart was fan - cy - free, Her heart was fan - cy -
tà, can - tan - do in li - ber - tà.
free, Her heart was fan - cy - free.

PETIT NOËL

(Little Noel)

Theophile Gautier
English version by
Margaret Aliona Dole

Emile Louis

Printed in the USA by G. Schirmer, Inc.

him smiles up - on his face sub - lime.
lui son vi - sa - - ge char - mant.
f
Bells, gay - ly chime a fes - tal song! The Christ is born! The
Clo - ches, ca - ril - lon - nez gaî - ment! Jé - sus est né, Jé -
p
Ped. Ped. Ped.
poco rit.
p a tempo
Christ is born! No warm, white cov-'ring in the
sus est né. Pas de cour - ti - nes fes - tonn -
a tempo
man - ger To keep the Babe from bit - ter cold;
né - es Pour pré - ser - ver l'enfant du froid;

On - ly the cob-webs for the stran - ger From raft-ers high they
Rien que des toi - les d'a - rai - gné - es Qui pen - dent des
p
poco rit.
a tempo
hang gray and old.
pou - tres du toit.
He on the fra-grant hay is
Il tremble sur la pail - le
sleep - ing, warm'd by the breath of friend - ly kine;
fraî - che, Ce cher pe - tit en - fant Jé - sus,
The ox - en gen - tle watch are keep - ing A - round the lit - tle
Et pour l'é - chauf-fer dans sa crè - che L'âne et le bœuf souf-
f

poco rit.
Un peu plus lent
Child di - vine.
flent des - sus.
The snow up - on the roof piles
La neige au chaume coud ses
poco rit.
pp
high - er,
fran - ges,
cresc.
But Heav-en o-pened where it fell.
Mais sur le toit s'ou-vre le ciel
cresc.
f
Hark! All in white the an-gel-choir
Et, tout en blanc, le chœur des an - - ges
poco rit.
To shep-herds
Chante aux ber -
poco rit.
f
f largo
ff
poco rit.
sing, No - ël! No - ël!
gers: No - ël! No - ël!
largo
poco rit.
sfz

THE PRAYER PERFECT

James Whitcomb Riley

Oley Speaks

*From Rhymes of Childhood, Copyright 1890, 1928. Used by special permission of the publishers, The Bobbs-Merrill Co.

Scat-ter ev-'ry care
Down a wake of an-gel wings Win-now-ing the
air. Dear Lord, kind Lord! Gra-cious Lord! I pray
Thou wilt look on all I love Ten-der-ly to-day.
f
mf
dim.
p
piacevole

mf
Bring un-to the sor - row-ing All re-lease from
p
pain, Let the lips of laugh - ter O - ver-flow a - gain,
cresc.
cresc.
mf
And with all the need - y O di-vide, I pray,— This vast trea-sure
mf

mf
of con-tent That is mine to - day! Dear Lord, kind Lord!
mf
dim.
dolce
Gra-cious Lord! I pray Thou wilt look on all I love Ten-der-ly to -
p
day.
p
mf

PER NON PENAR
(For My Heart's Peace)

Emanuele d'Astorga

English text by Nathan Haskell Dole

Allegro
mf

mf spigliato
Per non pe - nar non la-sce-rò d'a-mar,
For my heart's peace My love will nev-er cease!
pochiss. rit.
a tempo
p
mf

per non pe - nar non la_sce-rò d'a-mar; sem-pre co -
For my heart's peace My love will nev-er cease; Hum-bly de-
appena rit.
a tempo
p

Printed in the USA by G. Schirmer, Inc.

poco rall.
stan-te il va-go mi-o te-sor;
vo-ted to my de-lec-ta-ble one!
per non pe-
For my heart's
poco rall.
a tempo
pochiss. rit.
a tempo
mf
p
nar non la-sce-ró d'a-mar, no, no, sem-pre co-
peace My love will nev-er cease. Nay, nay, Faith-ful in
mf
p
stan-te il va-go mi-o te-sor, no, no, sem-pre co-
truth to my de-lec-ta-ble one! Nay, nay, Faith-ful in
mf
p
poco rall.
stan-te il va-go mi-o te-sor.
truth to my de-lec-ta-ble one!
poco rall.
a tempo
rall.
Fine
mf

a tempo
mp
Se ben cru - del l'a - do - re - ró fe - del, né ad al - tr' a -
Tho' he were cold, To him I'd faith - ful hold, And oth - er
a tempo
p
man - te mai vol - ge - rǒ il mio cor, se ben cru - del l'a - do - re - ró fe -
lov - ers my heart would ev - er shun. Tho' he were cold, To him I'd faith - ful
del, né ad al - tr' a - man - te mai vol - ge - rǒ il mio
hold, And oth - er lov - ers my heart would ev - er
largamente
D. C. dal segno
a tempo
cor, mai, no, mai, vol - ge - rǒ il mio cor. Per non pe -
shun, my heart would ev - er, ev - er shun. For my heart's
largamente
a tempo

TO A WILD ROSE

Hermann Hagedorn

Edward MacDowell
Transcribed by
R. H. Elkin

Printed in the U.S.A. by G. Schirmer, Inc.

cresc.
Droop, east! Die, west! Let my land rest. Woods, I
cresc.
woke your boughs, Hills, I woke your elf - throngs! Land, all thy hopes and
più cresc.
dim. e rit.
woes Rang from me in songs!
più cresc.
f
dim. e rit.
p
Come, oh, songs! Come, oh, dreams! In our house is deep rest,
p
sim.

Through the pines, gleams, gleams, Bright the gold west,
There the flutes shall cry, There the vi - ols weep, Laugh, my
dreams and sigh! Sing, and vig - il keep, "A -
wake, wild rose!"
mp
cantabile
rit.
p
Ped.

QUELLA BARBARA CATENA

(This Hard Bondage)

English version by Nathan Kaskell Dole

Francesco Ciampi

Printed in the USA by G. Schirmer, Inc.

rò,_ io di - rò che non dà pe - na, io di - rò,_ io di - rò,_ io di-
boast, I can boast it nev - er pains me, I can boast, I can boast, I can

rò_ che non dà pe - na, ma un so - a - ve e bel_ pia - cer,
boast it nev - er pains me,. Rath - er gives me keen de - light;
mf

rall.
no, no, i - o di - rò_ che non_ dà pe - na,
ay! ay! I_ can boast it nev - er pains me,
rall.
p
mf
p

a tempo
più p
poco rall.
ma un so - a - ve e bel_ pia - cer, e bel,_ e bel_ pia -
Rath - er gives me keen de - light! it gives me keen de -
a tempo
poco rall.
a tempo
mf
cer.
light!
Quel - la
This hard
a tempo
pochiss. rit.
a tempo
mf
p
mf
mp
bar - ba - ra_ ca - te - na che fa stra - zio del_ mio
bond - age that en - chains me, caus - ing an - guish in_ my

co- re io di - rò_ che non dà pe - na, io di - rò_ che non dà
bos-om, I can boast it nev - er pains me, I can boast it nev - er
pe - na, io di - rò_ che non_ dà pe - na, ma un so - a - ve e bel_ pia-
pains me, I can boast it nev - er pains me, Rath-er it gives me keen de-
cer, non fa stra - zio, non dà pe - na, quel - la bar - ba - ra_ ca -
light. This hard bond-age that en- chains me, I can boast it nev - er

poco rall.
te - na, io di - ro— che non dà pe - na, ma un so - a - ve e bel_ pia -
pains me, I can boast it nev - er pains me, Rath-er it gives me keen de -
poco rall.
a tempo
poco rall.
cer, e bel_ pia - cer, e bel_ pia -
light, a keen de - light, a keen de -
a tempo
mf
p
mf
poco rall.
p
cer.
light!
a tempo
mf
p
rall.
Fine

mf
Quel - la ri - a mor - tal fe - ri - ta che mi a - prì nel se - no A -
This in - cur - a - ble wound that kills me, In my heart by Love in -
a tempo
p
mo - re, che mi aprì nel se - no A - mo - re, di - rò pur che mi dà
flict - ed, In my heart by Love in - flict - ed, I can claim with life it
Da capo dal segno
vi - ta, che fa tutto il mio go - der, il mio go - der, il mio go - der.
fills me, Puts all thought of ill to flight, all ill to flight, all ill to flight!

ROMANCE

Paul Bourget
Translation by
M. Louise Baum

Claude Debussy

Moderato

Voice

Piano

p

L'âme é - va - po - rée et souf - fran - te, L'â - me dou - ce, l'âme o - do - ran - te Des lis di - vins que j'ai cueil - lis Dans le jar - din de ta pen - sée,

Ev - a - nes - cent breath of the lil - y, Ten - der fan - cies, O fra - grant spir - it of heav'n - ly lays, Which I in - hal'd 'mid gar - den - ways Of thy dear soul;

p *cresc.* *mf* *dim.*

Où donc les vents l'ont - ils chassée Cette âme a - do - ra - ble des lis?

Where is it fled on wings of air, Thy soul lil - y - pure, and so fair?

Printed in the USA by G. Schirmer, Inc.

Tempo rubato
pp meno mosso
N'est - il plus un par - fum qui res - te De la su - a - vi - té cé -
Is not one perfume still remain - ing Of all the heav'nly sweetness
pp meno mosso
les - - te Des jours où tu m'en - ve - lop - pais D'u - ne va -
reign - - ing In days when thou didst wrap me round With charm di -
Tempo I
p
mf
peur sur - na - tu - rel - le Fai - te d'espoir, d'amour fi - dè - le,
vine and all - per - vad - ing Fra - grant with hope, and love in - vad - ing,
mf
p
Ritenuto
dim.
p
De bé - a - ti - tude et de paix?
Bright with ho - ly joy, peace pro - found?
cresc.
dim.
p
pp

SELIGKEIT

(Bliss)

Ludwig Heinrich Christoph Hölty

Franz Schubert

Lustig (Merrily)
mf

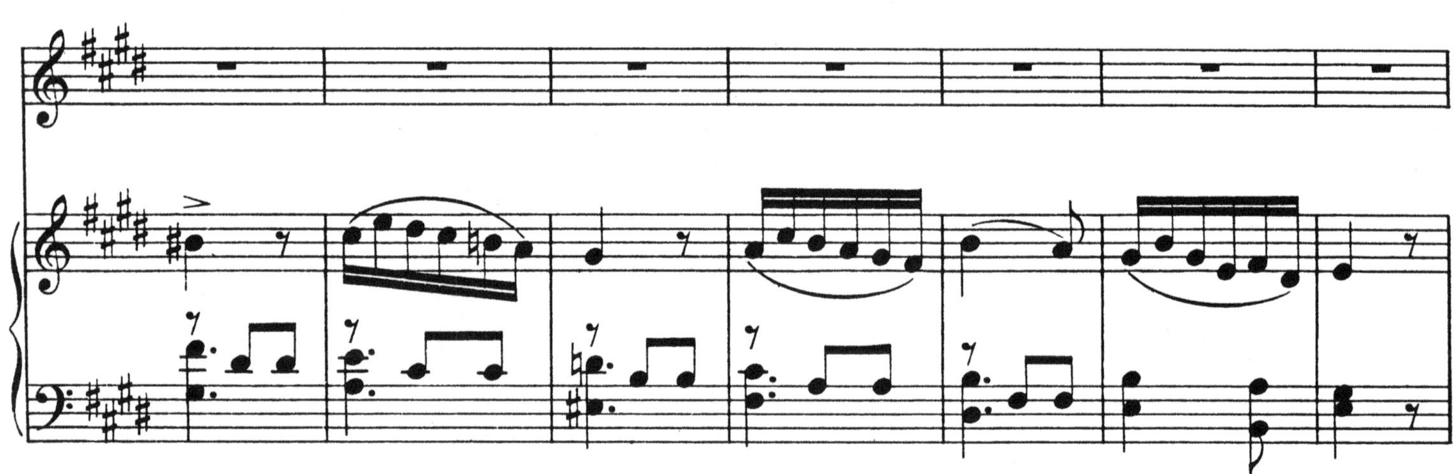

1. Freu-den son-der Zahl blüh'n im Him-mels-saal
2. Je-dem lä-chelt traut ei-ne Him-mels-braut;
3. Lie-ber bleib' ich hier, lä-chelt Lau-ra mir
1. Joy and peace and love reign in Heav'n a-bove:
2. Each one at his side has a heav'n-ly bride;
3. I would ra-ther stay here, with thee! says May,
p

Printed in the USA by G. Schirmer, Inc.

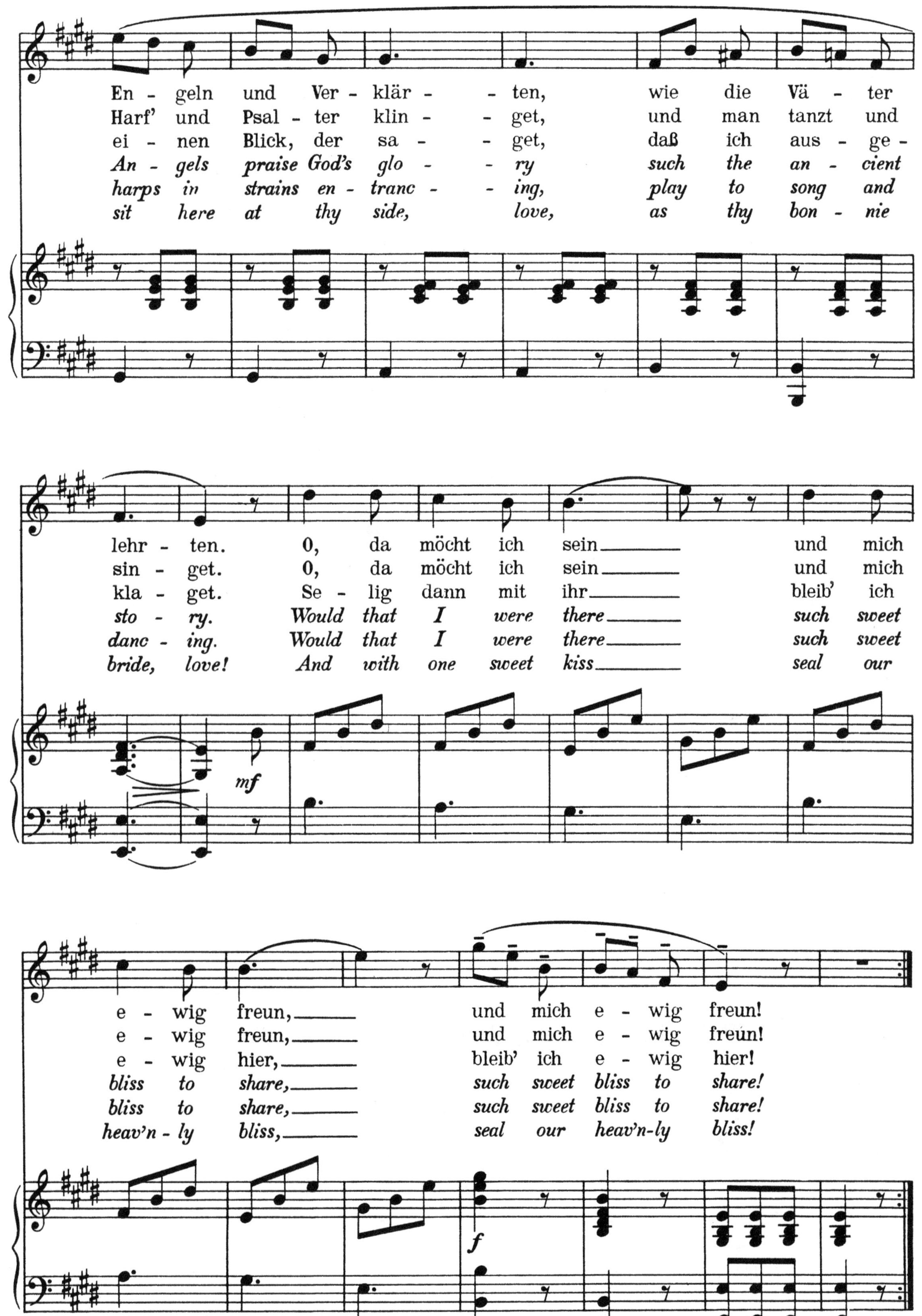
En - geln und Ver - klär - - ten, wie die Vä - ter
Harf' und Psal - ter klin - - get, und man tanzt und
ei - nen Blick, der sa - - get, daß ich aus - ge -
An - gels praise God's glo - - ry such the an - cient
harps in strains en - tranc - - ing, play to song and
sit here at thy side, love, as thy bon - nie
lehr - ten. O, da möcht ich sein und mich
sin - get. O, da möcht ich sein und mich
kla - get. Se - lig dann mit ihr bleib' ich
sto - ry. Would that I were there such sweet
danc - ing. Would that I were there such sweet
bride, love! And with one sweet kiss seal our
mf
e - wig freun, und mich e - wig freun!
e - wig freun, und mich e - wig freun!
e - wig hier, bleib' ich e - wig hier!
bliss to share, such sweet bliss to share!
bliss to share, such sweet bliss to share!
heav'n - ly bliss, seal our heav'n-ly bliss!
f

SOLVEJG'S SONG

Henrik Ibsen
English version by Arthur Westbrook

Edvard Grieg

Un poco Andante
PIANO
The win - ter may wane and the spring-time go by, the
Der Win - ter mag schei - den, der Früh - ling ver-geh'n, der
spring - time go by,
Früh - ling ver - geh'n,
The sum - mer too may van - ish, the
der Som - mer mag ver - wel - ken, das
year may die, the year may die;
Jahr ver-weh'n, das Jahr ver - weh'n;
But one day you'll re-turn, that in
du keh-rest mir zu-rü - cke, ge -
cresc.

truth — I know, in truth I — know, And here — I'll a-wait you as I
wiss, du wirst mein, ge - wiss, du wirst mein, ich hab' — es ver-spro - chen, ich
prom-ised long a-go, I prom-ised long a - go. —
har-re treu-lich dein, ich har-re treu-lich dein. —
(humming to herself:)
(vor sich hin summend:)
Ah! —
A —
f
p
pp
Allegretto con moto
pp una corda
simili
Tempo I
pp

p
May God guide your feet, if on earth still you rove, on
Gott hel - fe dir, wenn du die Son - ne noch siehst, die
p tre corde
earth still you rove. His bless-ed peace be yours, if in
Son - ne noch siehst. Gott seg - ne dich, wenn du zu
realms a - bove, in realms a - bove.
Fü - ssen ihm kniest, zu Fü - ssen ihm kniest.
poco animato
Faith-ful-ly I'll bide till a -
Ich will dei - ner har - ren, bis
poco animato
gain you draw near, a - gain you draw near, But if you wait in heav - en, at
du mir nah', bis du mir nah', und har-rest du dort o - ben, so
cresc.
f
cresc.

poco sostenuto
last I'll meet you there, at last I'll meet you there! Ah!
tref-fen wir uns da, so tref-fen wir uns da! A
poco sostenuto
Allegretto con moto
pp una corda
simili
Tempo I
tre corde
dim.

A SPIRIT FLOWER

B. Martin Stanton

Louis Campbell-Tipton

Printed in the USA by G. Schirmer, Inc.

sfz
ff
rit.
a tempo
black and star - - less night.
nichts als Nacht und Eis!
f
ff rit.
ff a tempo
mf
mf semplice
Down through the win-ter sun-shine snow-flakes came,
Dann fie - len Flo-cken nie-der, weiss und rein,
f
f
mf
f
mf patetico
All shim-m'ring, like to sil-ver but-ter-flies:
Wie Fal - ter flat-ternd hell im Sil-ber-schein;
f
mf
mf
f

★ Singers desiring to sing the *f*𝄪 should strike out the ♭ in the piano part

cresc.
rit.
seem - ing dead, a flo - - - wer!
Blüm - lein hold er - blü - - - hen!
ff
grandioso
Tempo I
f maestoso
Whose fragrance in my life shall e - ver be The
Und die-ser Blu-me Duft mir stets ver-blieb: Er
ff tutta forza
ff rall. f
p dolce (lingeringly)
pp
ten-der, sa-cred me-mo-ry of thee.
zeigt mir je - der - zeit dein Bild, mein Lieb!
pp
pp
mf
mp

WHEN DAISIES PIED

"Love's Labour's Lost"
William Shakespeare

Thomas Augustine Arne

In moderate time

mp *pp* *f* *p*

1. When dai - sies pied, and
2. When shep - herds pipe on

vi - o - lets blue, And la - dy smocks all sil - ver white, And cuck - oo buds of
oat - en straws, And mer - ry larks are plough - men's clocks, And tur - tles tread, and

yel - low hue, Do paint the mead - ows with ___ de - light:
rooks, ___ and daws, And maid - ens bleach ___ their sum - mer frocks:

f

Printed in the USA by G. Schirmer, Inc.

p
1-2. The cuck-oo then, on ev - 'ry tree, Mocks mar-ried men, mocks mar-ried men,
p
rit.
a tempo
p
cresc.
mocks mar-ried men; for thus sings he: Cuck-oo, cuck-oo, cuck-oo,
rit.
p
cresc.
f
p
f
p
cuck-oo, cuck-oo! O word of fear, O word of fear, Un -
f
p
f
rit.
pleas - ing to a mar - ried ear, un - pleas - ing to a mar - ried ear.
p
rit.

WHEN I WAS SEVENTEEN

H. Lilljebjörn
English version by Marion Bromley Newton

Swedish Folksong

*) These variants are by Madame Sembrich.

THE FIRST BOOK OF SOPRANO SOLOS

PART III

PREFACE

The First Book of Solos series has been compiled to meet requests of voice teachers who have expressed a need for more beginning vocal literature similar to the "Part I" and "Part II" books. This repertoire speaks to students who may have successfully sung songs from the *Easy Songs for Beginning Singers* series. Those students who have used *The First Book of Solos – Part I and Part II*, may still find that this level of song material is appropriate before venturing into the volumes of *The Second Book of Solos*. This new "Part III" may also suffice as a beginning book for certain students, or serve as a companion to "Part I" and "Part II." Since the level is the same for *The First Book of Solos – Part I, Part II and Part III*, a student can begin in any of the books.

The first two volumes were released in 1991 and 1993. Since then, some excellent songs have passed into the "Public Domain" category. It is significant that songs such as "The Green Cathedral," "Waters Ripple and Flow," "A Brown Bird Singing," "When I Think Upon the Maidens," "The Ships of Arcady," "May-Day Carol," and "The Time for Making Songs Has Come" have become available for young singers.

The anthologies in "Part III" contain 34 to 36 songs appropriate to specific voice types, and in suitable keys. The basic format provides songs of many styles from the baroque era into the 20th century. In addition to many familiar standard art songs, there are a number of unfamiliar gems, such as "The Bubble Song," the trilogy "At the Zoo," "Bluebird," "The Little Old Lady in Lavender Silk," "Maidens Are Like the Wind," "Sing a Song of Sixpence," and "When Big Profundo Sang Low C." In keeping with the original format, there are many American and British songs, as well as a good sampling of Italian, German and French art songs (with singable translations). Some favorites include "Invictus," "Come Back to Sorrento," "Vilia," and "I Walked Today Where Jesus Walked." As in the other books of the series, a few sacred solos are included. Many songs in "Part III" were previously obtainable in only sheet form or have been long out of print. In order to include songs represented by the 1916 to 1922 year span, several of the accompaniments and songs may prove to be a bit more of a challenge than in "Part I" and "Part II."

The First Book of Solos – Part III concludes this series of five books for each voice type, with no song duplication (*The First Book of Solos – Part I, Part II, Part III, The Second Book of Solos – Part I, Part II*). The number of songs in the twenty volumes totals 668. The average number of songs presented for each voice numbers approximately 167. This presents a wide smorgasbord of vocal literature for studio and performance use for student singers at most any age.

G. Schirmer is to be commended for allowing this series of vocal solos to grow substantially. Wherever I meet teachers who have used these many books, they express profound thanks for them, and acknowledge that their availability makes repertoire demands so much easier to manage. May you and your students enjoy the new choices made available in this anthology.

Joan Frey Boytim
June, 2005

CONTENTS

ART THOU TROUBLED?

English version by W.G. Rothery

George Frideric Handel
(1685-1759)

Larghetto
mp
mf
dim.
mp
p
Art thou troubled? Music will calm thee, Art thou
11
mp
weary? Rest shall be thine, rest shall be
15
mp
thine. Music, source of all gladness,

poco cresc.
Heals thy sad - ness At her shrine, Mu - sic,
mf
poco cresc.
mu - sic, ev - er di - vine, Mu - sic,
mp
p
rall.
a tempo
mu - sic call - eth With voice di - vine.
mf
dim.
Fine

39
mp
When the wel - come spring is smil - ing, all the earth with flow'rs be -
p
43
guil - ing, Af - ter win-ter's drear - y reign,
mp
Sweet-est mu - sic doth_at -
cresc.
p
cresc.
47
tend_her, Heav'n - ly har - mon - ies doth_lend her,
mf
Chant - ing
mf
50
prais - es in her train,
f
chant - ing prais - es in her train.
rall.
f
D.S. al Fine

MY MOTHER BIDS ME BIND MY HAIR

(Bind' auf dein Haar)

Anne Hunter

Franz Joseph Haydn
(1732-1809)

up my sleeves with rib - ands rare, And lace my bod - ice blue,
ro - sen-ro - ten Schleifen licht, so schmück' Dein Mie - der fein,
fz
Tie up my sleeves with rib - ands rare, And lace, and
mit ro - sen-ro - ten Schlei-fen licht, so schmück', so
fz
fz
lace my bod - ice blue.
schmück' Dein Mie - der fein.
For
Willst
why, she cries, sit still and weep, While oth - ers dance and
trau - ern Du, mein Kind, al - lein, weil Al - les tanzt so

play? A - las! I scarce can
gern? Ach, a - ber ach das
rf
p
go or creep, While Lu - bin is a - way. A -
Her - ze mein seufzt: weh! mein Lieb' ist_ fern! Ach,
rit.
mp
las! I scarce can go or creep, while Lu - bin_ is a - way, while
a - ber ach, das Her - ze mein seufzt: weh! mein Lieb' ist_ fern! mein
p
mf
dim.
slen - p - tan - do
pp
Lu - bin is_ a - way, is a - way, is a - way.
Lieb', mein Lieb' ist fern! Ist so fern! Ist so fern!
slen - tan - do
pp

mf
'Tis sad_ to think the days are gone, When those_ we love are near! I
O schö-ne Zeit, da Er_mir nah', den ein-zig ich_ge-liebt, ich
mf
sit___up-on this mos-sy stone, And sigh when none can hear,
si-tze auf dem Stei-ne da und seuf-ze schwer be-trübt.
fz
I sit_ up-on this mos-sy stone, and sigh,_ And sigh when none can_
Ich si-tze auf dem Stei-ne da und seuf-ze, seuf-ze schwer be-
fz
fz
hear.
trübt.
And while I spin my
Ich spin-ne, doch ich

flax - en thread, And sing my sim - ple lay, The
weiss es kaum; ich sing' mein klei - nes Lied, doch
rf
p
vil - lage seems a - sleep or dead, Now Lu - bin is a - way, The
Al - les tot und wie ein Traum, seit Er, der Liebste schied, doch
rit.
mp
vil - lage seems a - sleep or dead, now Lu - bin is a - way, now
Al - les tot und wie ein Traum, seit Er, der Lieb - ste schied, seit
p
mf
dim.
slen - p tan - do pp
Lu - bin is a - way, is a - way, is a - way.
Er, der Lieb - ste schied, seit Er schied, seit Er schied.
p
slen - tan - do
pp

for my mother

BLUEBIRD

Rudolph Schirmer
(b. 1919)

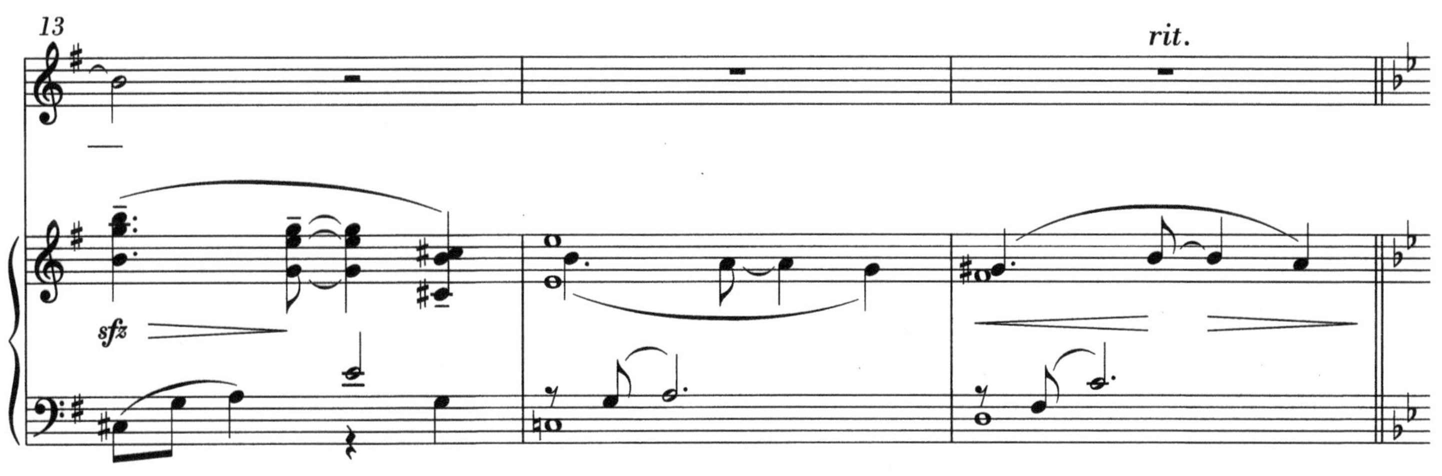
13
rit.
sfz

16
Meno mosso
But when my blue - bird is sing - ing a - bove me,
p

20
There'll come a cloud in the sky,

24
poco cresc.
Steal - ing my blue - bird and him who would love me,
poco cresc.

28
Leav - ing me on - ly a sigh.
32
mp
Don't you know
mf
mp
36
poco allarg.
Love will go Where the blue - bird
più f
40
a tempo
rall.
flies?
3
p
ppp morendo

A BROWN BIRD SINGING

Royden Barrie

Haydn Wood (1892-1959)

13
rit.
a tempo
Could go wing - ing To you, to you.
16
mf
pp legato
poco rit.
19
a tempo
p
All through the night - time my lone-ly heart is sing-ing Sweet-er songs of love than the
p
22
poco rit.
brown bird ev - er knew, Sweet-er songs of love than the brown bird ev - er knew.

a tempo
mp
mf
poco rit.
Would that the song of my heart could go a-wing - ing, Could go a-wing - ing To
you, to you.
a tempo
p più tranquillo
All through the night - time my
lone - ly heart is sing - ing
meno mosso
pp ten.
mp
opt.
Sweet - er songs of love than the
ten.
pp
a tempo
opt.
brown bird ev - er knew.
ppp

FOR MY SOUL THIRSTETH FOR GOD

from *Psalm 42*

Felix Mendelssohn
(1809-1847)

16
for the liv - ing God,
For my soul
20
thirst - eth for God, yea, for the liv
23
- ing God,
for God, yea,
sf
l.h.
p
27
for the liv - ing God.
When shall I come to ap - pear be -
sf
p
pp
r.h.

31
sf
fore the pres-ence of God? when shall I come to ap - pear be -
sf
p
35
cresc.
fore God's pres - ence, be - fore, be -
cresc.
f
f
38
fore God's pres - ence?
cresc.
p
42
When shall I come to ap - pear,
sf
p
cresc.

45
when shall I come to ap -
48
pear, to ap - pear be - fore God's
p
pp
51
pres - ence?
sf
cresc.
54
f
For my soul thirst - eth for God, for my
f

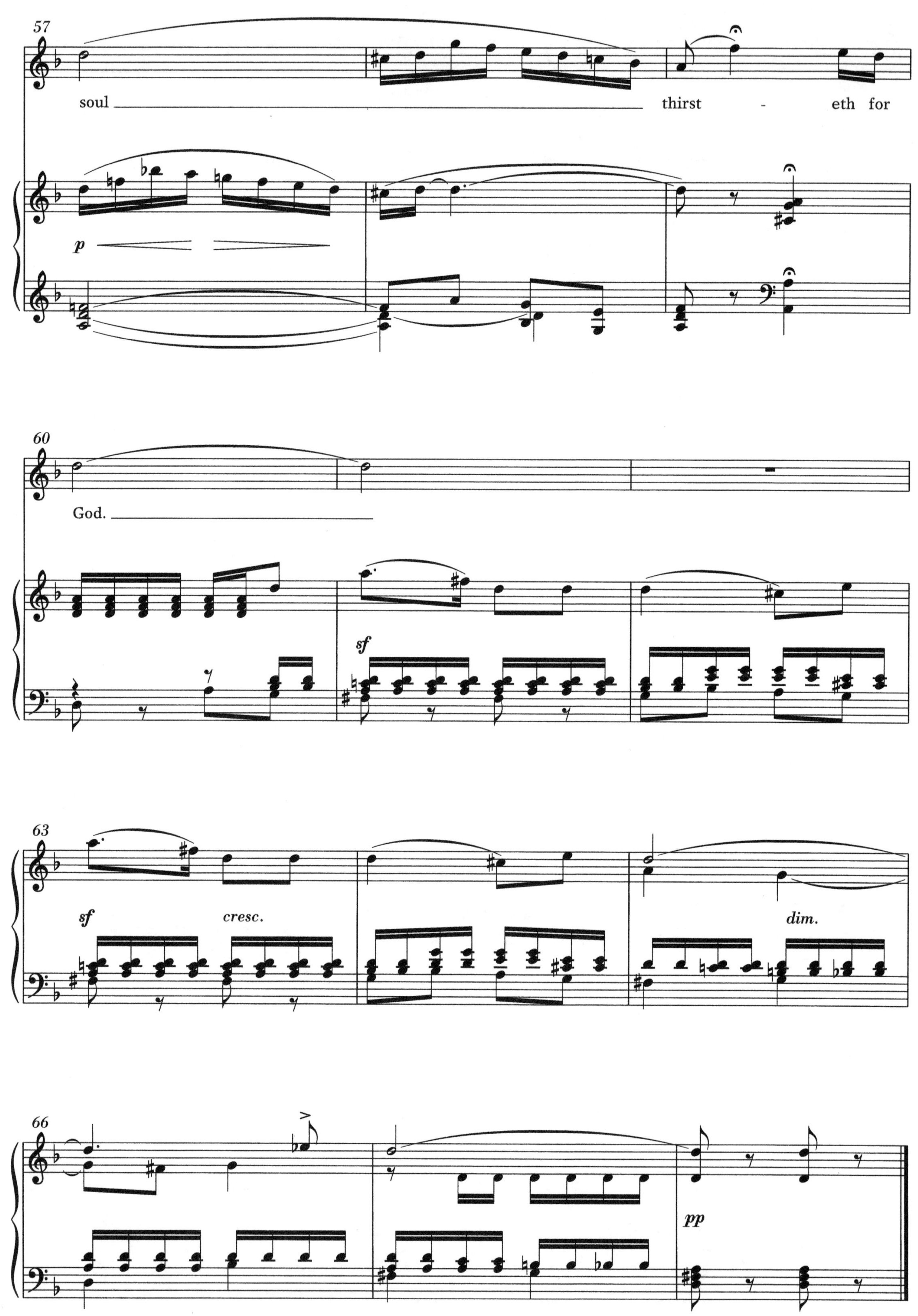
57
soul
thirst - eth for
p
60
God.
sf
63
sf
cresc.
dim.
66
pp

THE GREEN CATHEDRAL

Gordon Johnstone

Carl Hahn
(1874-1929)

13
leaves in love join hands a - bove And
15
arch your pray'r and mine; With -
17
in its cool depths sa - cred, The
19
priest - ly ce - dar sighs, And the

21
fir and pine lift arms di - vine Un -
23
poco rall.
p
slightly faster
to the pure blue skies. In my dear green ca -
p
Ped.
26
the - dral, There is a flow - ered seat. And choir loft in
30
poco rit.
p a tempo
branch - ed croft, where song of bird - hymns sweet; And I
tr
p

33
like to dream at eve - ning, When the
35
stars its arch - es light, That my
37
Lord and God treads its hal - low'd sod, In the
p
39
cool, calm peace of night, That my
p

41
opt.
pp
Lord and God treads its hal - low'd sod, In the
pp
43
poco rall.
cool, calm peace of night.
p softly
45
*Hum
Hum
due Ped.
49
Hum
Hum

* Or "ah"

I WILL LAY ME DOWN IN PEACE

(O God of my righteousness)

Maurice Greene
(1696-1755)

9
mf
for it __ is __ thou, 'tis thou, _ O __ Lord, that mak'st me to dwell,
f
to

rall. a tempo

11

mf pp

dwell _ in __ safe - ty, to dwell in safe - ty, to dwell in safe - ty;

mf

13

mf

I will lay __ me __ down _ in __

p

15
pp
pp
peace, _ will lay _ me _ down _ in _ peace, _ will lay me
pp
pp

17
down in peace, _ and take my rest, and take _ my _ rest: _
mf

19
mf
f
mp
mf
for it _ is _ thou, 'tis thou, _ O _ Lord, that mak'st me to dwell in safe - ty, for it is
p
mf
mp

22
f
mp
mf
thou, 'tis thou, O Lord, 'tis thou, O Lord, that mak'st me to dwell in
p
mf

24
p
mf
safe - ty, that mak'st me to dwell in safe - ty, to dwell in
mf
p

26
rall.
p
pp
safe - ty, to dwell in safe - ty, mak'st me to dwell, in safe - ty.
p
pp

I WILL SING OF THY GREAT MERCIES

from *St. Paul*

Felix Mendelssohn
(1809-1847)

Recitative
So they, be-ing fill-ed with the Ho - ly Ghost, de - part-ing thence de-lay'd not, and
f
4
Con moto ♪ = 92
preach - ed the word of God with joy - ful-ness. I will sing of Thy great
p
7
mer - cies, O Lord, of Thy mer - cies, O Lord, my

11
Sa - viour, I will sing of Thy great
15
mer - cies, O Lord, and of Thy faith - ful - ness
cresc.
p
19
ev - er - more. I will sing of Thy great
p
23
mer - cies, O Lord, I will sing of Thy great
sf

27
mer - cies, O Lord,
and of Thy faith - ful-ness,
f
31
and of Thy faith - ful-ness,
and of Thy faith - ful - ness
cresc.
35
ev - er - more.
p
I will sing of Thy great
sf
p
39
mer - cies, O Lord,
and of Thy faith - ful - ness

43
ev - er - more, and of Thy faith - ful - ness
dim.
mf
p
47
ev - er - more, ev - er -
52
more, ev - - - er -
56
more.

IN MEINEM GARTEN DIE NELKEN

(My treasured flowers are dying)

Emanuel von Geibel

Robert Franz
(1815-1892)

13
Flam - men, die ich be - wacht so
cher - ished that on my hearth once
15
cresc.
gern, san - ken in A - sche zu -
shone, sank in - to ash - es and
cresc.
17
sam - men, denn du bist
per - ished, for thou art
19
fern.
gone.
melodia ben marcato

Die Welt ist mir ver - dor - ben, mich
The world is bare, be - night - ed, now
grüsst nicht Blu - me, nicht Stern, mein
I am left all a - lone, my
Herz ist lan - ge ge - stor - ben, denn du bist
heart is long a - go blight - ed, for thou art
fern.
gone.
cresc.
dim.

LOVE AMONG THE DAFFODILS

Edward Teschemacher

Eric Coates
(1886-1957)

allargando
rall.
The glad birds ca - rolled gai - ly This hap - py A - pril
colla voce
Animato
song.
cresc. molto
"Hey, ho!
Der - ry down dey! Life in spring-time's sweet and mer - ry, When you tread the
rall.
sun - lit hills,
a tempo
Pick - ing beau - ti - ful daf - fo - dils!"
8va

37
ff
mf
sim.
42
mp delicato
As we roamed down the hill-side, A stran-ger
mp
46
ten.
rall.
we did meet, He car-ried bows and ar-rows, 'Twas Cu-pid young and
51
mp meno mosso
accel.
sweet! He wound-ed us so sore-ly, But we had
mf
mp
ten. ten. ten.

55
allargando
ne'er a fear, Who would not wel - come Cu - pid,
58
rall.
dim.
When A - pril time is here!
Animato
dim.
colla voce
62
cresc. molto
"Hey, ho! Der-ry down dey!
66
Life in spring-time's sweet and mer - ry, Hey, ho! Der - ry down dey!

70
cresc.
rit. molto
Life in spring-time's sweet and mer - ry,
cresc.
allargando
a tempo animato
73
ten.
ten.
Hey, ho! Der-ry down dey! Life in spring-time's sweet and mer - ry,
colla voce
77
rall.
accel.
cresc.
When you tread the sun - lit hills, Find - ing
8va
cresc.
81
allargando
Presto
love 'mid the daf - - - fo - dils!"

MAMAN, DITES-MOI
(Mother, please explain)

Harmonized by
Jean-Baptiste Weckerlin
(1821-1910)

English version by Sigmund Spaeth

Un poco allegretto
p
Ma - man, di - tes - moi ce qu'on
Moth - er, please ex - plain, what is
p
sim.

5
sent quand on ai - me, Est - ce plai - sir, est - ce tour -
love? Won't you tell me? Does one feel joy, or is it

9
ment?
sad?
Je suis tout le jour dans u - ne
How am I to know what of

13
peine ex - trê - me, Et la nuit je ne
late be - fell me? For now my life no
17
sais com - ment... Quel mal peut nous cau - ser un a -
more is glad. Oh, tell me, is lov - ing al - ways
sfz
21
pp
poco rit.
mant? Si quel-qu'un près de nous sou - pi - re,
bad? Sup - pose a gen - tle swain is sigh - ing,
26
Que faut - il lui di - re?
Should I be de - ny - ing?

30
p
Un ber - ger bien fait, Plus beau que l'a - mour, Vint d'un air dis -
Not long since, to me Came a shep - herd fair, Hand-some as could
p
35
cret Me ju - rer l'au - tre jour Qu'il m'ai - mait bien.
be, And prompt-ly he did swear That he loved me well.
40
p
cresc.
Je ne dis rien, Je ne dis rien. Mais s'il re -
How could I tell? How could I tell? But if he
p
cresc.
45
rit.
vient en - cor m'en dire au - tant, Que faire a - lors, ma - man? Que
comes and says the same a - gain, What should I an - swer then? What

50
faire a - lors, ma - man?
should I an - swer then?
8va
10
10
53
p
C'est le ber - ger le plus par - fait du vil -
No one in the vil - lage com - pares with his
p
sim.
58
la - ge, Tout ce qu'il dit, tout ce qu'il fait,
beau - ty; What - ev - er he may do or say
63
Est si sé - dui - sant, que sans peine on s'en - ga - ge,
Is so full of charm, that one feels it a du - ty

67
Tant il a de char - mes, d'àt - traits. Quel mal nous peut
Al - ways to let him have his way. Why should we not
sfz
72
pp
poco rit.
cau - ser un a - mant? Si près de nous son cœur sou -
love for just a day? When such a gen - tle heart is
77
pi - re, Que faut - il lui di - re?
sigh - ing, Should I be de - ny - ing?
82
p
Ce ber - ger char-mant, plus beau que l'a - mour, D'un air bien dis -
Thus it is with me, Since this shep-herd fair, Hand-some as could

87
cresc.
cret M'a ju - ré l'au - tre jour qu'il m'ai - mait bien.
be, Did come to me and swear That he loved me well.
cresc.
92
p
Je ne dis rien, Je ne dis rien. Mais s'il re -
How could I tell? How could I tell? But if he
p
cresc.
97
rit.
vient en - cor m'en dire au - tant, Que faire a - lors, ma -
comes and says the same a - gain, What should I an - swer
101
rall.
man? Que faire a - lors, ma - man?
then? What should I an - swer then?
8va
10
10

MAY-DAY CAROL

English Folksong (Essex)

Transcribed and Harmonized by
Deems Taylor
(1885-1966)

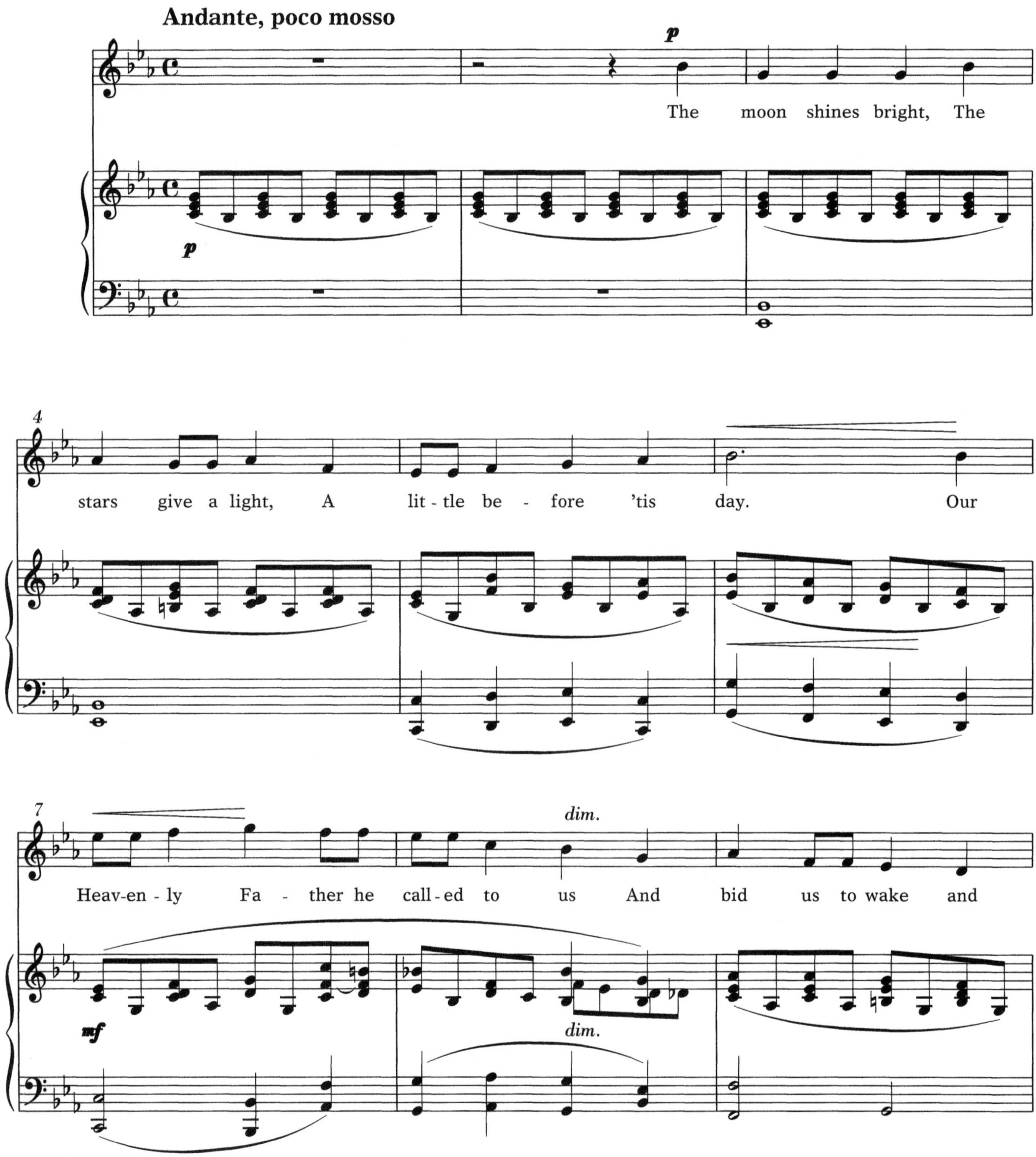

Andante, poco mosso
p
The moon shines bright, The
p
4
stars give a light, A lit - tle be - fore 'tis day. Our
7
dim.
Heav-en - ly Fa - ther he call - ed to us And bid us to wake and
mf
dim.

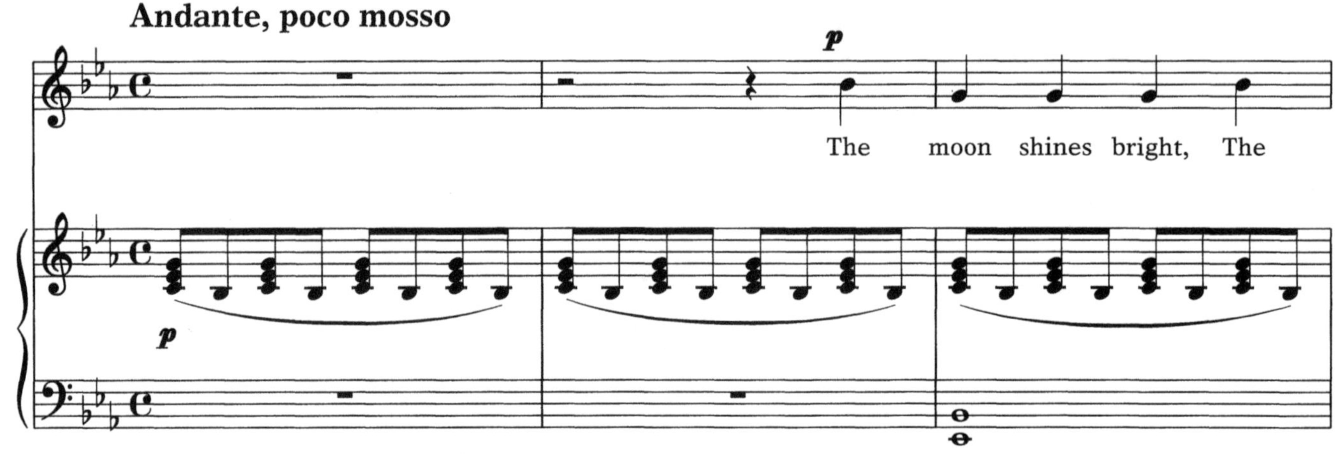

10
poco rit.
p
a tempo
pray. A - wake, a - wake, O pret-ty, pret-ty maid, Out
p
13
mf
of your drows - y dream, And step in - to your
mf
16
rit.
p
a tempo
dair-y be-low, And fetch me a bowl of cream.
p
mp
20
p
rit.
a tempo
If not a bowl of your sweet cream, A
p
3
Ped.
Ped.

23
mf
cup to bring you cheer; For the Lord knows where we shall
mf
26
p rit.
meet a - gain To be may - ing an - oth - er year. I
29
a tempo
cresc.
been a - ram - bling all this night, And some time of this
p
32
mf
dim.
day, And now, re - turn - ing back a - gain, I
f
dim.

35
p
brought you a branch of May.
p
mf
appassionato
38
rit.
pp
A
cresc.
f
molto dim.
p
41
a tempo
branch of May I brought you here, And at your door I
pp
44
mf
dim.
stand. 'Tis no-thing but a sprout, but well bud-ded out By the
cresc.
mf
dim.

47
rall.
p
a tempo
work of Our Lord's hand. My song is done, and I
pp
50
must be gone, No long - er can I stay, So it's
rit.
pp subito
53
a tempo
God bless you all, both great and small, And send you a joy - ful
pp subito
colla voce
56
pp
molto lento
May, And send you a joy - ful May.
pp
colla voce
sempre pp
3
Ped.
*

THE MERRY WIDOW WALTZ

English words by Adrian Ross

Franz Lehár (1870-1948)
Arranged by H.M. Higgs

throw ing Light a - - bove, While the
sway - - ing Tune is say - - ing Love, love, love!
And the feet of danc - - ers Sound it
as they go Don't you hear them say My

rit.
dear, I love you so! And with the mu-sic's
rit. colla voce
Valse lento
chime, My heart is beating time, As if to give a
sign That it would cry Be mine, be mine! Though our
pp
lips may say no word, Yet in the heart a voice is heard,

That seems to whisper soft and low, I love you so!
animato
Love that hov - - ers O - - ver lov - - ers Speaks
p animato
in song,
In the fin - - ger's
Clasp that lin - - gers Close and long

allargando
And the mu - - sic an - - - - swers Sway - - ing
allargando
to and fro
Tell - - ing you, It's
Allegro
true, it's true I love you so!
f

MOTHER SORROW

English version by Joan Boytim

Edvard Grieg
(1843-1907)

Con moto
p
1. Have you seen my lit - tle one with eyes so bright and clear.
2. Jes - us mild, my lov - ing child why were you tak - en a - way?
Of - ten have we watched him yet he is no long - er here.
Did they need an - oth - er an - gel? For man - kind to - day.
Ah so emp - ty cold and bare.
Have they giv'n him shin - ing wings?

13
Stands his cra - dle small and a - las what
Do bright robes a - dorn him? Help me now, this
molto legato
16
pp
dark de - spair up - on my heart de - scend - eth.
sor - row to bear, and give me tears to mourn him.
pp
20
rit.
23
1.
a tempo
2.
molto rit.
pp

à Mignon Palmer

IL NEIGE
('Tis snowing)

Hermann Bemberg
English version by R.H. Elkin

Hermann Bemberg
(1861-1931)

15
cresc.
dim.
f
vec des airs fri - leux, En fer - mant les yeux. Il nei - ge, il
get - ting how to trill, All has grown so still. 'Tis snow - ing, 'tis
cresc.
dim.
f
20
poco rall.
nei - ge, Tout est cou-vert d'un blanc man - teau de nei -
snow - ing, The world's a - sleep be - neath a snow - y co -
colla voce
24
Tempo I
- ge!
- ver!
29

34
Il nei - ge, il nei - ge! Com-me il fait froid Par les
'Tis snow - ing, 'tis snow - ing! 'Tis drear and lone, And the
38
durs fri-mas, Qui gla - cent, qui gla - cent nos â - mes d'ef -
winds that moan Are turn - ing, are turn - ing our ve - ry hearts to
42
p
froi! Et se sen-tant très mal-heu-reux, Les jeu-nes cœurs
stone! And lov - ers sad, wea-ry of pain, Sigh for the spring's
p
46
a - mou-reux Deux à deux Se ré - chauf - fent entr'
ge - nial reign, When all hearts wake to love a -

50
f
dim.
eux. Il nei - ge, il nei - ge, Tout pas - se, tout s'ef -
gain. 'Tis snow - ing, 'tis snow - ing, All fades a - way be -
f
dim.
54
poco rall.
Tempo I
fa - ce sous la nei - ge!
neath a snow - y co - ver!
colla voce
59
opt.
p
Il nei - ge! Il
'Tis snow - ing! 'Tis
poco rit.
a tempo
64
poco rit.
nei - ge!
snow - ing!
8va
colla voce
dolce
8va
Ped.
*

à Madame Moreau-Sainti

NUIT D'ÉTOILES
(Lovely night of stars)

Théodore de Banville
English version by Susanna Myers

Claude Debussy
(1862-1918)

Allegro
mf
Nuit d'é - toi - les, Sous _ tes
Love - ly night of stars, with _ your
pp
una corda

7
voi - les, Sous ta bri ___ se et tes _ par - fums, Tris - te ly -
veil - ing light, And your soft ___ breeze like _ a lyre, Wist - ful sigh -

14
f
p dim.
re Qui sou - pi - re, Je rêve aux a - mours _ dé - funts, Je
ing, Love un - dy - ing, I dream _ of those _ now gone, I
f
p

21
p
mf un peu animé
rêve aux _ a - mours dé - funts.
La se - rei - ne mé-lan-co - li - e Vient é -
dream ___ of those now ___ gone.
In the spell of gen - tle night _ Comes to
p
mf
27
clore au fond de mon cœur,
Et j'en - tends
l'â - me de _ ma mi - e Tres - sail-
me a mys - ti - cal hour,
List - 'ning long,
I feel the soul of my love ___ Trem - bling
32
un poco rit.
lir dans le bois rê - veur.
here in dream - ing bow'r.
37
p
rit.
a tempo
Nuit d'é - toi - les,
Sous _ tes voi - les,
Love - ly night of stars,
With ___ your veil - ing light
[p]

41
Sous ta bri - se et tes par - fums,
And your soft breeze like a lyre,
45
Tris - te ly - re Qui sou - pi -
Wist - ful sigh - ing, Love un - dy -
49
re, Je rêve aux a - mours dé - funts, Je
ing, I dream of those now gone, I
f
54
animé
rêve aux a - mours dé - funts. Je re - vois à no - tre fon -
dream of those now gone. Once a - gain I may be -

59
sempre cresc.
tai - ne Tes re - gards bleus com-me les cieux; Cet - te ro - se,
hold In your eyes the blue of the skies, And this rose
cresc.
63
f
c'est ton ha - lei - ne,
Breathes your soul,
Et ces é - toi - les
And the stars are
67
sont tes yeux.
love in your eyes.
f
71
pp
Nuit d'é - toi - les, Sous tes
Love - ly night of stars, With your
pp
una corda

74
dim.
voi - les, Sous ta bri se et tes par -
veil - ing light And your soft breeze like a
78
fums, Tris - te ly - re Qui sou
lyre, Wist - ful sigh - ing, Love un -
8va
82
morendo jusqu' à la fin
pi - re, Je rêve aux a - mours dé -
dy - ing, I dream of those now
loco
86
ritenuto
pp dim.
funts, Je rêve aux a - mours dé - funts.
gone, I dream of those now gone.
pp dim.

PRAISE

George Herbert

George Dyson
(1883-1964)

Largamente 𝅗𝅥 = ca. 60
mf
f
Let all the world
in ev - 'ry cor - ner sing
marcato
My God and King.
mf
The heav'ns are not too high,
His praise may thith - er fly,

12
mf
mf
The earth is not too low, His prais - es there may grow. Let all the
mf
16
marcato
world in ev - 'ry cor - ner sing My God, my God and
20
f
tenuto
King.
The Church with psalms must shout,
mf
f
24
mp
No door can keep them out; But, a - bove
mf

27
espressivo
all, the heart Must bear, must bear the long - est
espressivo
30
f
part. Let all the world in ev - 'ry cor - ner sing
molto
f
34
crescendo
My God, my God, my God and
crescendo
ff
ff
38
King.
f
ff

THE POOL OF QUIETNESS

Grace Wallace

Thomas Vincent Cator

Lento ma non troppo

Andante sostenuto

p

You are the pool of quiet-ness Where my high drift-ing star is pearled;

mf *p* *rit.*

cresc.

You are the breeze in the asp-en leaves Noon has yellow'd and curled.

rit. molto *a tempo*

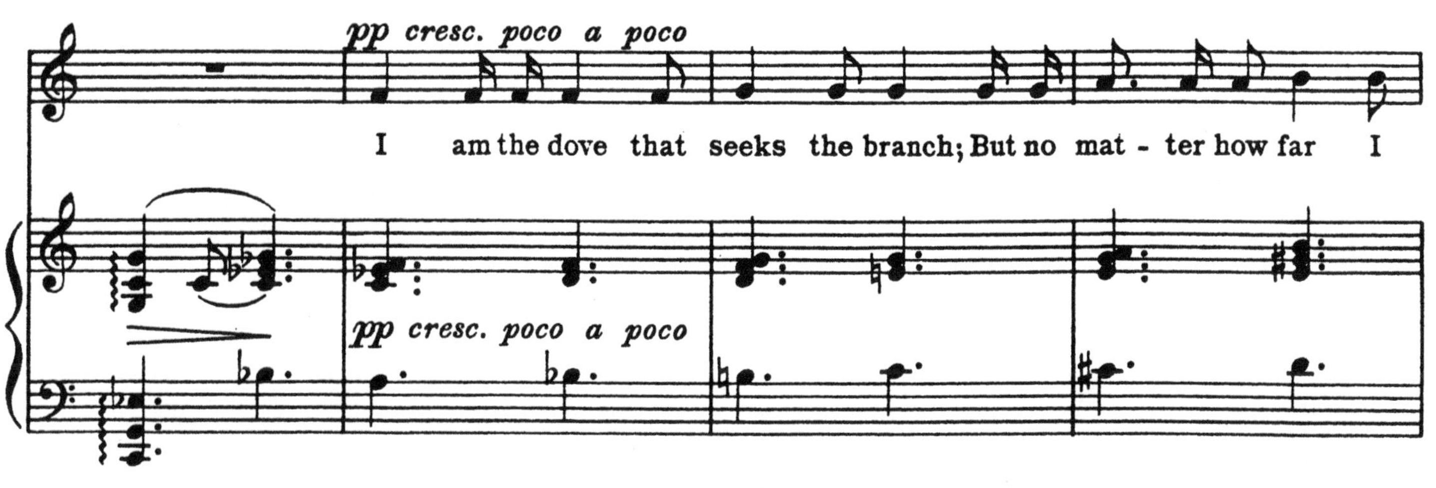
pp cresc. poco a poco
I am the dove that seeks the branch; But no mat - ter how far I
pp cresc. poco a poco

ff
p rall.
fly, I shall re-turn to rest in your palm By - and - by,
ff
p rall.

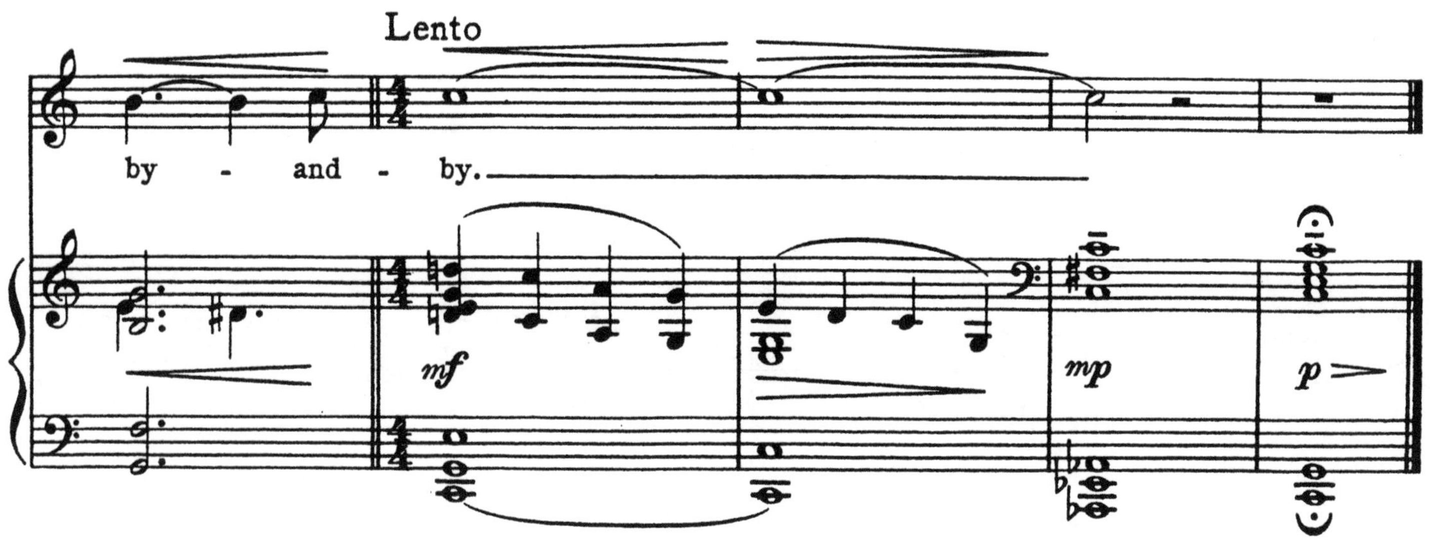
Lento
by - and - by.
mf
mp
p

RIDENTE LA CALMA
(How calm is my spirit)

Wolfgang Amadeus Mozart
(1756–1791)

*appoggiatura possible

13
mor. Ri - den - te la cal - ma nell' al - ma si
cend! How calm is my spir - it, from sor - row re -
17
de - sti; Ne re - sti più se - gno di sde - gno e ti -
leas - ed, The An - gel of peace on my heart doth des -
21
mor, Ne re - sti più se - gno di sde - gno e ti -
cend! The An - gel of peace on my heart doth des -
25
mor, di sde - gno e ti - mor.
cend! My heart doth des - cend.
f
p
cresc.
f

29
Tu vie - ni, frat - tan - to, a strin - ger mio
'Tis thou who hast shown me the path - way to
p
33
be - ne, Le dol - ce ca - te - ne sí
heav - en oh! lead me, oh! guide me, be -
36
gra - te al mio cor, sí gra - te al mio
lov'd to the end, be - lov'd to the
fp
39
cor, sí gra - te al mio cor. Ri - den - te la
end, be - lov'd to the end. How calm is my
fp
p

43
cal - ma nell' al - ma si de - sti, nell'
spir - it, from sor - row re - leas - ed, From
46
al - ma si de - sti;
sor - row re - leas - ed;
cresc.
f
49
Ne re - sti un se - gno di sde - gno e ti -
The An - gel of peace on my heart doth des -
p
53
mor. Ri - den - te la cal - ma nell' al - ma si
cend! How calm is my spir - it, from sor - row re -

57
de - sti, Ne re - sti più se - gno di
leas - ed, The An - gel of peace on my
60
sde - gno e ti - mor, Ne re - sti più
heart doth des - cend! The An - gel of
63
se - gno di sde - gno e ti - mor, di sde - gno e ti -
peace on my heart doth des - cend! My heart doth des -
f
p
67
mor.
cend!
cresc.
f

DER SANDMANN
(The Sand-Man)

Gustave Herrmann Kletka
English version by Frederic Field Bullard

Robert Schumann
(1810-1856)

Nicht zu schnell
pp
p
Zwei fei - ne Stief - lein hab' ich an,
Two dain - ty lit - tle shoes I wear;
mit wun - der - wei - chen Söhl - chen dran;
Their soles are soft be - yond com - pare;
ein Säck - lein hab' ich hin - ten auf, husch! tripp' ich rasch die
A sack up - on my back I bear; Hush! now I'm trip - ping
fp

16
Trepp' hin-auf.
up the stair.
Und
And
cresc.
19
wenn ich in die Stu - be tret die Kin - der be - ten
when I reach the nurs - 'ry there, And find the chil - dren
22
ihr Ge - bet:
all at pray'r,
von
Two
fp
25
mei - nem Sand zwei Kör - ne-lein streu' ich
grains of sand of smal - lest size I drop
fp
sfp

28
auf ih - re Äu - ge-lein,
in - to their lit - tle eyes;
da
And
sfp
una corda
32
rit.
schla - fen sie die gan - ze Nacht in Got - tes und der
then they sleep the whole night long, While God doth watch and
36
a tempo
Eng - lein Wacht.
an - gels throng.
pp
tre corda
40
p
Von mei - nem Sand zwei Kör - ne-lein
When of my sand two ker - nels fine

44
streut' ich auf ih - re Äu - ge - lein:
I drop with - in the chil - dren's eyen;
48
den from - men Kin - dern soll gar schön ein fro - her Traum vor -
To lov - ing chil - dren 'tis a sign That they shall sleep with
fp
52
ü - ber - geh'n. Nun risch und rasch mit
dreams di - vine. Then up and off, with
cresc.
56
Sack und Stab nur wie - der jetzt die Trepp' hin - ab.
sack and stick A - down the stairs with foot - steps quick!

59
Ich kann nicht län - ger müss - ig steh'n,
I can no long - er lin - ger here
fp
fp
63
muss heut' noch zu gar Vie - len geh'n–
Must go to ma - ny chil - dren dear.
da
E'en
sfp
sfp
una corda
68
rit.
nickt ihr schon und lacht im Traum, und öff - ne - te doch mein Säck - lein
now in dreams you're smil - ing back, And yet I have hard - ly oped my
pp
73
a tempo
kaum.
sack!
dim.

SE MERITAR POTESSI

(If only by deserving)

English version by Nathan Haskell Dole

Domenico Bruni
(1758-1821)

più for - tu - na - to al - lor, più for - - tu -
What bless - ed for - tune were mine! What bless - - ed
na - - to al - lor; ma sí fe - li - ce sor - te per
for - tune were mine! Yet were this bliss de - nied me, Should
me non è ser - ba - ta, quest' al - ma non è
cru - el loss be - tide me, No oth - er love should

na - ta per— sì— fe - li - ce a - mor,— quest' al - ma non— è—
guide me Down life's dark sad de - cline!— No oth - er love— should
rall.
a tempo
na - ta per— sí— fe - li - ce a - mor. Se me - ri - tar po-
guide me Down life's dark sad— de-cline. If on - ly by de-
rall.
a tempo
tes - si, ca - ra, gli af - fet - ti tuo - i, sa -
serv - ing, I— might claim thy af - fec - tion, My

re - i de' nu - mi̮i - stes - si
dear one, by Fate's di - rec - tion,
più for - tu - na - to,
What bless - ed for - tune,
più for - tu - na - to,
What bless - ed for - tune,
più for - tu - na - to̮ al-
What bless - ed for - tune were
lor, più for - tu - na - to̮ al - lor.
mine! What bless - ed for - tune were mine!
rall.
rall.

SOUND THE FLUTE!

William Blake

Celius Dougherty
(1902-1986)

Lit-tle Boy, Full of Joy; Lit-tle Girl, Sweet and small;
sempre pp
Cock does crow, So do you; Mer-ry voice, In - fant noise;
Mer-ri-ly, Mer-ri-ly, Mer - ri-ly, To wel - come in the Year.

più pp
Lit-tle Lamb, Here I am; Come and lick My white neck;
ppp
dim.
Let me pull Your soft Wool; Let me kiss Your soft face:
dim.
rit.
Mer-ri-ly, Mer-ri-ly, Mer - ri-ly, We wel-come in the Year.
rit.

SPLEEN

Paul Verlaine
English version by Harry Goldby

Lady Dean Paul Poldowski
(1880-1932)

Andante
rall.
lamento
p
Les
All
sans traîner
pp
[p]
l.h.
ben legato
dim.
5
ro - ses é-taient tou-tes rou - ges et les lier - res é-taient tout
red were the ros - es, all red and the i - vy was black, all
pp
8
f avec désespoir
noirs Chè - re, pour peu que tu te bou - ges re -
black. Dear one with ev - 'ry move you make, des -
p
suivez

11
rall.
très calme
pressez un peu
rit.
nais - sent tous mes dé - ses-poirs
pair, des - pair takes on new life.
Le ciel é - tait trop bleu trop
The sky was too blue and too
rubato
suivez
14
dim.
ten - dre La mer trop verte et l'air trop doux
ten - der, the sea too green, the air too soft.
17
avec inquiétude
sub. p
de plus en plus intense
Je crains tou-jours ce qu'est d'at - ten - dre quel-que fuite a - tro - ce de
It is my con-stant dread and fear that one day you may dis - ap -
agitato
leggiero
suivez
20
pressez
cresc.
vous. Du houx à la feuil - le ver -
pear. Of hol - ly with its glist - 'ning
dim. leggiero morendo

22
agitato
cresc.
ni - e et du lui-sant buis Je suis las
leaves and of box-woods sheen I am tired
suivez
25
f
et de la cam-pagne in - fi - ni - e et de tout
of the coun-try-side with its vast - ness and of all things
cresc.
rall.
appassionato
ff
rinforzando
28
rit.
a tempo
fors! de vous hé - las.
ex - cept you a - las.
31
rall.
dim.
p
pp
pp sostenuto
ppp

SUR LA TERRASSE DE SAINT GERMAIN
(On the Terrasse of Saint-Germain)

André Alexandre
English version by Harry Goldby

Félix Fourdrain
(1880-1923)

Allegro marcato

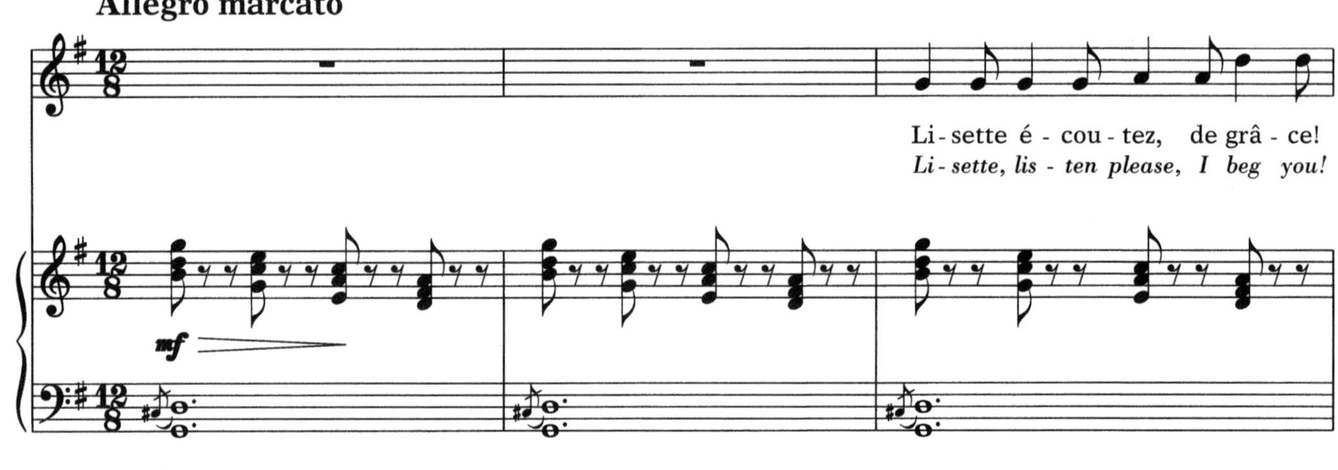
Li-sette é - cou - tez, de grâ - ce!
Li - sette, lis - ten please, I beg you!
mf

4
Non! je vais à Saint-Ger-main, Re - trou-ver sur la Ter-ras - se ce - lui qui m'au-ra de-main.
No! I'm off to Saint - Ger-main, there to meet on the Ter-ras - se him who'll be all mine this day.

7
f
p

10
Du Ma - ré - chal de No - ail - les
Ser - ving the Mar - shal of No - ail - les
12
mf
C'e - tait un sim - ple gre - na - dier. Pa -
He is a sim - ple gre - na - dier. It
14
raît que dans les ba - tail - les
seems that in all the bat - tles
p
16
f
Il s'en - tend bien à co - gner!
He holds his own blow for blow!
f

[Meno]
pp
Nous cau-sons d'a-mour en-
There we'll speak of love to-
pp
sem - ble, Sur un banc, tout à l'é - cart.
geth - er, on a bench, off to the side.
Mon cœur bat, mon re-gard
My heart beats, my be-ing
trem - ble Aux flam-mes de son re - gard.
trem - bles at those flames seen in his eyes.
poco rit.
Il jure d'ê-tre fi - dè - le, Il ju - re d'ê-tre fi - dè - le,
He swears that he'll be faith - ful, He swears on oath that he'll be faith - ful,

35
Tempo I
Tan - dis qu'au loin j'a - per - çois
While I can see on a branch
mf
p
37
un oi - seau qui bat de l'ai - - - le
a small bird that flut - ters its wings
opt.
39
Et s'en - fuit vers les grands bois.
Then flies off to - wards the woods.
f
3
6
41
p en cedant
Vers les grands bois.
To - wards the woods.
p

STAR VICINO
(Let me linger near thee)

English version by May Byron

Anonymous*

*Previously attributed to Salvator Rosa (1615-1673).

21
go di - let - to, di - let - to d'a - mor, più va -
- ness should sev - er My spir - it from thine, should sev -
p
26
go di - let - to d'a - mor!
er my spir - it from thine!
cresc.
mf
31
Star lon -
But I
tr
dim.
dolce
36
tan - o dal ben che si bra - ma, È d'a - mor - e il più
wan - der in si - lence and sor - row, And I dream of the

41
mes - to do - lor! È d'a - mor - e il più
sweet - ness of yore, And I wak - en to
45
tr
mes - to do - lor! è il più
know that the mor - row Will
49
mes - to do - lor, più mes - to do -
bring thee no more, to know that the
p
cresc.
53
lor! il più mes - to do - lor!
mor - row Will bring thee no more!

to Jim

TO A LITTLE CHILD

Clara Edwards
(1887-1974)

ten.
slightly slower
in time
14
dew.
Then the
lark
will
wa - ken
you
8va
ten.
cresc.
17
less slow
mf
The
dim.
20
blue of the night is in your eyes, The gold of dawn in your
23
hair.
Your voice is soft as the breeze which sighs, The

26
pressing on
smile that comes with glad sur - prise And lights your face so
29
ten.
f
broadly
as at the beginning
fair, Spreads sun - shine ev - 'ry - where.
8va
ten.
f
32
34
mp
The sea - gulls fly toward the
mp

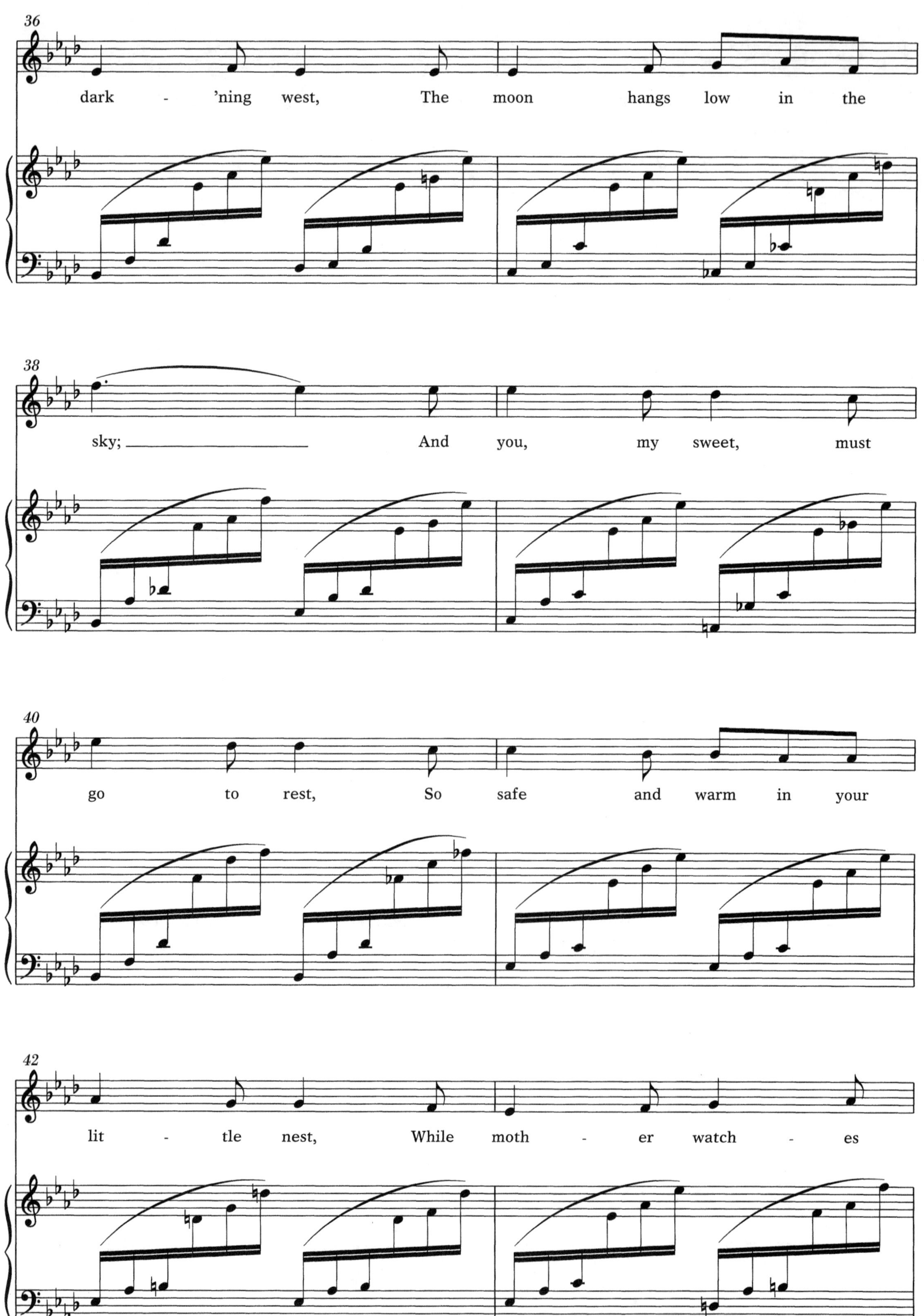
36
dark - 'ning west, The moon hangs low in the
38
sky; And you, my sweet, must
40
go to rest, So safe and warm in your
42
lit - tle nest, While moth - er watch - es

44
ten.
expressively
as at first
nigh
As she sings you a lull - a - by.
8va
ten.
expressively
mp
47
Lull - a - by,
49
fading away
Lull - a -
dim.
51
by.
8va
loco

THE TIME FOR MAKING SONGS HAS COME

Hermann Hagedorn

James H. Rogers
(1852-1933)

hop, and soon the bees will hum.
ten.
ten.
ten.
Lento e mesto
mf
Long was the win - ter, but our lips were dumb;
Long un - der
mp
mp
mf
mf
ben sostenuto
snow our loy - al dreams have lain;
p
dolce
Sure-ly the time for mak - ing songs has come,

sempre dolce
Now that the spring is in the air a - gain!
agitato
sffz
The spring! with bu - gles and a
f subito e stridente
f
p
slentando
mf ben moderato
rum - bling drum! O build - ers of high mu - sic out of
p
mf sonore
mf più animato
pain! Now is the time with
più animato
mf
cresc.

sempre cresc.
sing - ing to make vain The boasts of kings in pan - de -
ff
mo - ni - um!
ff
f
Sure - ly the time for mak - ing songs has
l.h.
l.h.
come!
8
ff con forza, non troppo vivo

LA VEZZOSA PASTORELLA
(In the cool and dewy morning)

English version by Nathan Haskell Dole

Domenico Bruni
(1758-1821)

Allegro non tanto

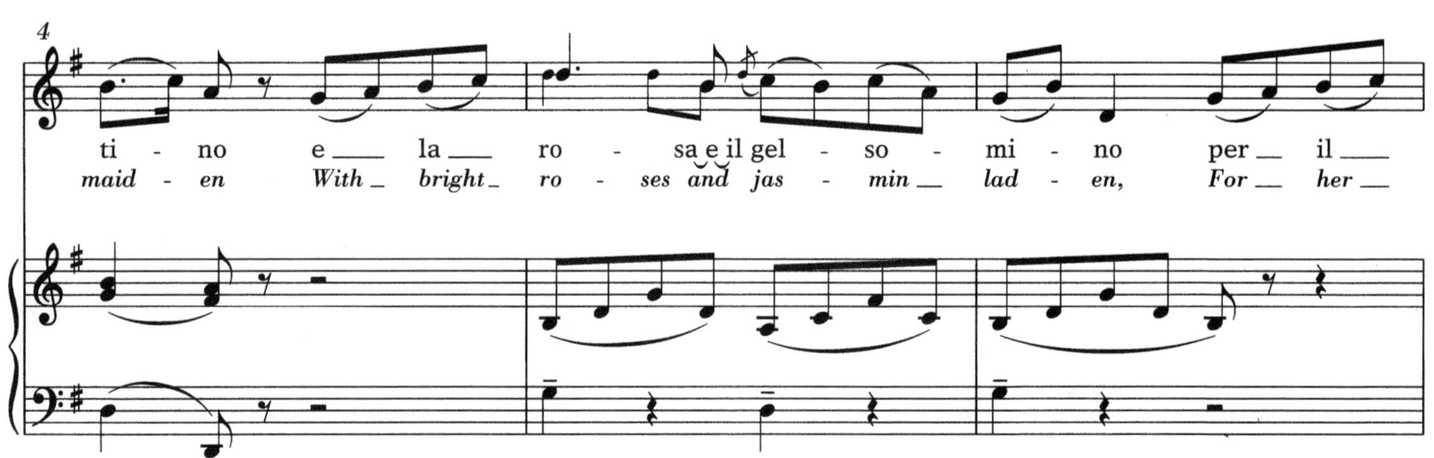

10
ti - no e la ___ ro - sa e il gel - so - mi-no per il ca - ro, per il
maid - en, With bright_ ro - ses and jas - min_ lad-en For her dear - est, for her
14
ca - ro, per ___ il ca - ro ___ suo pa-stor; ma qual cru - da, a-cer - ba
dear - est, For ___ her dear - est ___ one de-signed; Oh the cru - el dis - il -
18
pe - na gli si de - sta in mez - zo al co - re; più non
lu - sion, Which no words could suf-fice ______ to meas - ure! She can
21
ve - de il su - o pa - sto - re, più non tro - va il su - o te -
no - where be - hold ___ her treas - ure, All in vain her Love she tried to

24
sor, più non tro - va il su - o te - sor, no, no, non
find! All in vain her love she tried to find. A - las, her
27
rall.
a tempo
p
tro - va il su - o te - sor! La vez - zo sa pa - sto -
shep-herd she no-where can find! In the cool and dew - y
p
30
rel - la va co - glien - do in sul mat - ti - no e la
morn - ing Fares the love - ly shep - herd maid - en, With bright
33
ro - sa e il gel - so - mi - no per il ca - ro suo pa - stor, va co -
ro - ses and jas - min lad - en, For her dear - est one de-signed; Fares the

37
glien - do in sul mat - ti - no e la ro - sa e il gel - so -
love - ly shep - herd maid - en With bright ro - ses and jas - min
40
mi - no per il ca - ro, per il ca - ro, per il
lad - en For her dear - est, for her dear - est, For her
43
ca - ro suo pa - stor, per il ca - ro suo pa -
dear - est one de - signed, for her dear - est one de -
46
largamente
rall.
stor, per il ca - ro suo pa - stor.
signed, for her dear - est one de - signed!
mf
f

VILIA

from *The Merry Widow*

Franz Lehár
(1870-1948)

English words by Adrian Ross

Simplified Piano Arrangement by H.M. Higgs

Allegretto
There
once was a Vil - ia, A witch of the wood, A hunt - er be -
held her a - lone as she stood. The spell of her beau - ty up -

15
rit.
on him was laid; He looked and he longed for the mag - i - cal maid!
pp
21 pp a tempo
For a sud-den trem - or ran, Right through the love-be-wil-dered man,
pp
25 mf rit.
a tempo
p
And he sighed as a hap-less lov - er can. "Vil - ia, O Vil - ia! the
mf
p
con Ped.
31
witch of the wood! Would I not die for you, dear, if I could?

37
p
Vil - ia, O Vil - ia, my love and my bride!" Soft - ly and sad - ly he
p
43
f
f
sighed. "Vil - ia, O Vil - ia, the witch of the wood!
mf
f
49
f
poco lento
pp
Would I not die for you, dear, if I could? Vil - ia, O Vil - ia, my
f
pp
55
rit.
love and my bride!" Soft - ly and sad - ly he sighed.

61
Allegretto
64
The wood - maid - en smiled, and no an - swer she gave, But
69
beck - oned him in - to the shade of the cave; He nev - er had
74
rit.
known such a rap - tur - ous bliss, No maid - en of mor - tals so

79
pp a tempo
sweet - ly can kiss! As be-fore her feet he lay, she van-ished in the wood a -
pp
84
rit.
mf
way, And he called vain-ly till his dy - ing day!
mf
89
p
"Vil - ia, O Vil - ia! the witch of the wood, Would I not die for you,
p
con Ped.
95
dear, if I could? Vil - ia, O Vil - ia, my love and my bride!"

101
p
Soft - ly and sad - ly he sighed
mf
"Vil - ia, O Vil - ia! the
107
f
witch of the wood, Would I not die for you, dear, if I could?"
113
poco lento
pp
"Vil - ia, O Vil - ia, my love and my bride!"
rit.
Soft - ly and sad - ly he
119
sighed, Sad-ly he sighed, Vil - ia.
mf
p
morendo
ppp

WATERS RIPPLE AND FLOW

Czecho-Slovak Folksong
English version by Deems Taylor

Harmonized by Deems Taylor
(1885-1966)

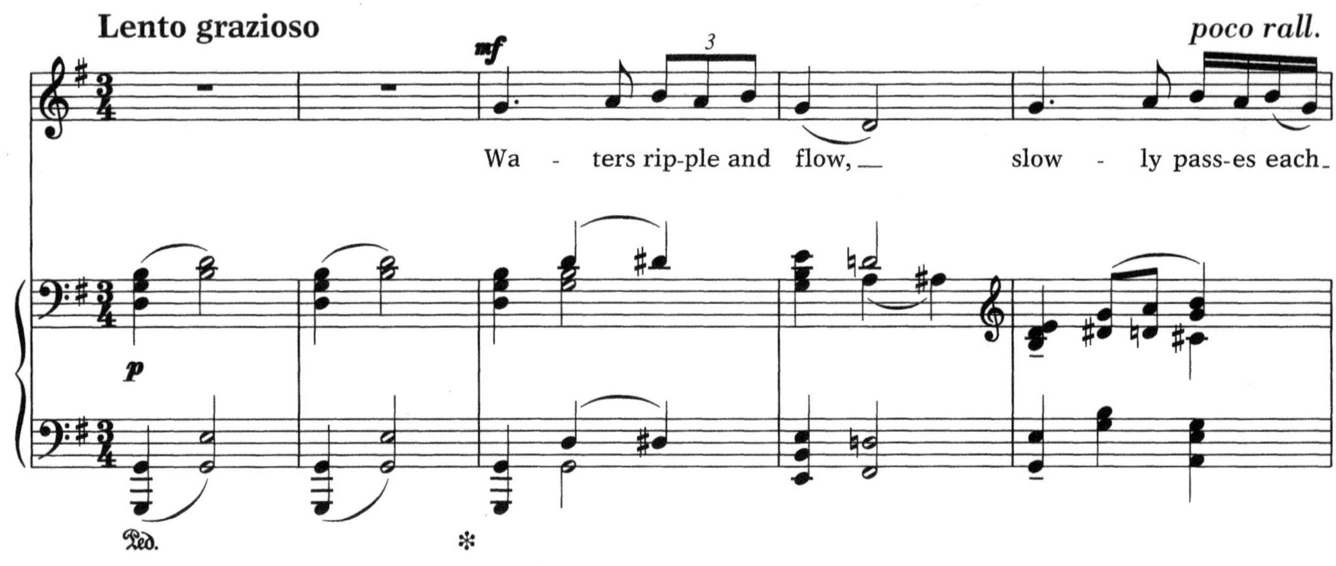
Lento grazioso
poco rall.
mf
Wa - ters rip-ple and flow, slow - ly pass-es each
p

6
a tempo
poco rall.
a tempo
day; Faith - less lov-er of mine, stay no long-er a - way;

11
mf
mp
rall.
a tempo
Faith - less lov-er of mine, stay no long-er a - way.
mf
p
colla voce
mf

rall.
a tempo
poco rall.
16
mf
p
mp
Dear one, well dost thou know why fond lov-ers must
21
a tempo
poco rall.
a tempo
part: Where - fore fal-ters thy faith? why so tim-id thy heart?
26
f
p
rall.
a tempo
Where - fore fal-ters thy faith? Why so tim-id thy heart?
mf
colla voce
con pedale
30
mp
rall.
dim.

a tempo
34
mp
Dear - est lov-er, come back; end the vi-gil I
mp
37
keep. Thine, the key to my heart,
40
poco rall.
mine, with-out thee to weep. Thine, the key to my
f
f
43
p
rall.
a tempo
heart; mine, with-out thee to weep!
l.h.
p
colla voce
p

46
mf
When the moun-tain shall turn,
con pedale
49
when the vic-t'ry is thine,
Then my hap-pi-ness
52
rall.
dawns, then shall free-dom be mine;
mp
55
Then my hap-pi-ness dawns, then shall free-dom be
rall.
p

58
a tempo
mine.
mf
61
mf
più f
64
f
rall.
Sostenuto
68
f
Lo, the moun-tain has turned, now the vic-t'ry is
f

71
thine; Now my hap - pi - ness dawns,
3
74
ff
now shall free-dom be mine; Now my hap - pi - ness
3
ff
77
rall.
molto rit.
p
dawns, now shall free-dom be mine, now shall free-dom be
p
colla voce
81
a tempo
mine!
pp
Ped.
*
Ped.
*

WELCOME, PRETTY PRIMROSE

Ciro Pinsuti
(1829-1888)

Allegretto moderato

p legg. elegante

p

5

p

8

meno mosso

p

1. Wel-come, pret - ty prim - rose flow'r, That
2. Gaz - ing on thee, ear - ly flow'r, I

sf *p* *pp legg.*

11

comes _ when _ sun - shine comes, When rain-bows arch the sil - ver
seem _ to ___ hear the spring, That calls the sun-shine ev - 'ry

pp legg. *p*

14
show'r Of ev - 'ry cloud that roams, Of
hour, And tells the bird to sing! And
p
sostenuto
p
17
rall.
rit.
ev - 'ry cloud that roams. I
tells the bird to sing! And
p
a tempo
20
joy to see thy prom - ise bloom, That tells of spring's new
as I dream, my dream is rife With thoughts a - kin to
23
rinf.
f
day; And in my thoughts a - far I roam O'er
thee, Of glad spring life, a sweet spring life, That's
f

26
cresc.
sun - ny haunts a - way!
ver - y dear to me.
Wel - come!
cresc.
p
29
un poco string.
Wel - come!
Wel - come! prim - rose flow'r!
Allegretto moderato
32
p elegante
Wel - come, pret - ty prim - rose flow'r! To me thy com - ing
p legg. scherzando
35
seems To wake a - gain the spring - time hour, With

38
sun - shine in its dreams!
Ah!
mf
41
f
Ah!
f
44
p stacc. con grazia
rit.
f
opt.
Wel-come, pret-ty, pret-ty, pret-ty, pret-ty, prim-rose flow'r, With sun - shine in its
p stacc. con grazia
f
col canto
1.
2.
47
a tempo
dreams!
dreams!
sf
sf

WHEN JESUS WALKED ON GALILEE

Warren Charles Klein

Clara Edwards
(1887-1974)

mf
new hope smiles a - gain. The heav - y du - ty and the
mf
task That bur - den with their care Grow light - er if we
on - ly ask God's help in si - lent prayer.
più f
mp
As

soft - ly as the spring-tide's breath, Sweet qui - e - tude creeps
p
segue (sostenuto sempre)
in, And scenes in old - en Naz - a -
mf
reth Ap - pear a - bove earth's din. There comes a
mf

still - ness in the heart, Quite like that calm, clear sea
When Je - sus bade the storm de - part, And walked on
Gal - i - lee!
dim.
p
pp
8

to Miss Phyllis Neilson-Terry

THE WILLOW SONG

William Shakespeare
from *Othello*

Samuel Coleridge-Taylor
(1875-1912)

a tempo
knee Sing wil - low, wil - low, wil -
pp
poco rit.
a tempo
- low:
rit.
The
f
dim.
a tempo
fresh streams ran by her, and mur - mur'd her

31
moans, Sing wil - low, wil-low, wil - low: Her
35
rit.
a tempo
salt tears fell from her, and soft - en'd the stones;– Sing wil - low,
40
rit.
wil - low, wil - - - low:
pp
44
più mosso
f
Sing all a green wil - low must be my gar -
mf
f

(slower)
mp
land. Let no - bo - dy blame him, his scorn I ap - prove,
(still slower)
I call'd my love false love; but what said he then? Sing
pp
rall. poco a poco
wil - low, wil - low, wil - - -
- low.

UNDER THE GREENWOOD TREE

William Shakespeare
from ***As You Like It***

Thomas Augustine Arne
(1710-1778)

throat, And tune his mer-ry note Un-to the
sweet bird's throat: Come hith-er, come
hith-er, come hith-er, come hith-er, come hith - er, come hith-er, come hith-er, come
hith - er!

27
p
Here shall he see No en - e - my But win - ter and rough
p
30
weath - er, Here shall he see No en - e - my But
33
win - ter and rough weath - er, Here shall he see No
36
en - e - my But win - ter, but win - ter and rough

40
weath - er, rough weath - er, but win - ter and rough weath - er.
f
43
rit.
p
a tempo
Un - der the green - wood tree Who
p
47
loves to lie with me And tune his mer - ry
50
note Un - to the sweet bird's throat, And tune his mer - ry
tr
tr

54
note Un - to the sweet bird's throat, Come hith - er, come
58
hith - er, come hith - er, come hith - er, come
61
rit.
hith - er, come hith - er, come hith - er, come hith - er, come hith - er, come hith - er, come
64
[a tempo]
hith - er!